Chapter 16: Caring for Aging Dogs

What they will experience is very much like what we humans experience when falling asleep under anesthesia during a surgical procedure.

Once the second stage drug has been injected, the entire process takes about 10 to 20 seconds, at which time the veterinarian will then check to make certain that the dog's heart has stopped.

There is no suffering with this process, which is a very gentle and humane way to end a dog's suffering and allow them to peacefully pass on.

4. When to Help a Dog Transition

The impending loss of a beloved dog is one of the most painfully difficult and emotionally devastating experiences a canine guardian will ever have to face.

For the sake of our faithful companions, because we do not want to prolong their suffering, we humans will have to do our best to look at our dog's situation practically, rather than emotionally, so that we can make the best decision for them.

They may be suffering from extreme old age and the inability to even walk outside to relieve themselves, and thus having to deal with the indignity of regularly soiling their sleeping area, they may have been diagnosed with an incurable illness that is causing them much pain, or they may have been seriously injured.

Whatever the reason for a canine companion's suffering, it will be up to their human guardian to calmly guide the end-of-life experience so that any further discomfort and distress can be minimized.

5. What to Do If You Are Uncertain

In circumstances where it is not entirely clear how much a dog is suffering, it will be helpful to pay close attention to your dog's behavior and keep a daily log or record so that you can know for certain how much of their day is difficult and painful for them, and how much is not.

When you keep a daily log, it will be easier to decide if the dog's quality of life has become so poor that it makes better sense to offer them the gift of peacefully going to sleep.

During this time of uncertainty, it will also be very important to discuss with your veterinarian what signs of suffering may be associated with the dog's particular disease or condition, so that you know what to look for.

Often a dog may still continue to eat or drink despite being upset, having difficulty breathing, excessively panting, being disoriented or in much pain, and as their caring guardians, we will have to weigh their love of eating against how much they are really suffering in all other aspects of their life.

Obviously, if a canine guardian can clearly see that their beloved companion is suffering throughout their days and nights, it will make sense to help humanely end their suffering by planning a euthanasia procedure.

We humans are often tempted to delay the inevitable moment of euthanasia, because we love our dogs so much and cannot bear the anticipation of the intense grief we know will overwhelm us when we must say our final goodbyes to our beloved fur friend.

Unfortunately, we may regret that we allowed our dog to suffer too long, and could find ourselves wishing that if only we humans had the same option, to peacefully let go, when in our own lives, we find ourselves in such a position.

6. Grieving a Lost Friend

Some humans do not fully recognize the terrible grief involved in losing a beloved canine friend. There will be many who do not understand the close bond we humans can have with our dogs, which is often unlike any we have with our human counterparts.

Your friends may give you pitying looks and try to cheer you up, but if they have never experienced such a loss themselves, they may also secretly think that you are making too much fuss over "just a dog".

Chapter 16: Caring for Aging Dogs

For some of us humans, the loss of a beloved dog is so painful that we decide never to share our lives with another, because we cannot bear the thought of going through the pain of loss again.

Expect to feel terribly sad, tearful and yes, depressed because those who are close to their canine companions will feel their loss no less acutely than the loss of a human friend or life partner.

The grieving process can take some time to recover from, and some of us never totally recover.

After the loss of a family dog, first you need to take care of yourself by making certain that you keep eating and getting regular sleep, even though you will feel an almost eerie sense of loneliness.

Losing a beloved dog is a serious shock to the system, which can also affect your concentration and your ability to find joy or want to participate in other activities that may be part of your daily life.

During this early grieving time you will need to take extra care while driving or performing tasks that require your concentration as you may find yourself distracted.

If there are other dogs or pets in the home, they will also be grieving the loss of a companion, and may display this by acting depressed, being off their food or showing little interest in play or games. Therefore, you need to help guide your other pets through this grieving process by keeping them busy and interested, taking them for extra walks and spending more time with them.

Many people do not wait long enough before attempting to replace a lost pet and will immediately go to the local shelter and rescue a deserving dog. While this may help to distract you from your grieving process, this is not really fair to the new fur member of your family.

Bringing a new pet into a home that is depressed and grieving the loss of a long time canine member may create behavioral problems for the new dog who will be faced with learning all about their new home while also dealing with the unstable, sad energy of the grieving family.

A better scenario would be to allow yourself the time to properly grieve by waiting a minimum of one month to allow yourself and your family to feel happier and more stable before deciding upon sharing your home with another dog.

The grieving process will be different for everyone and you will know when the time is right to consider sharing your home with another canine companion.

7. The Rainbow Bridge Poem

"Just this side of heaven is a
place called Rainbow Bridge.
When an animal dies that has been
especially close to someone here,
that pet goes to Rainbow Bridge.
There are meadows and hills for all of our special friends
so they can run and play together.
There is plenty of food, water and sunshine,
and our friends are warm and comfortable.

All the animals who had been ill and old
are restored to health and vigor;
those who were hurt or maimed
are made whole and strong again,
just as we remember them in our dreams
of days and times gone by.
The animals are happy and content,
except for one small thing;
they each miss someone very special to them,
who had to be left behind.

They all run and play together,
but the day comes when one suddenly stops
and looks into the distance.
His bright eyes are intent; His eager body quivers.
Suddenly he begins to run from the group,
flying over the green grass,
his legs carrying him faster and faster.

You have been spotted,
and when you and your special friend finally meet,
you cling together in joyous reunion,
never to be parted again.

The happy kisses rain upon your face;
your hands again caress the beloved head,
and you look once more into the trusting eyes
of your pet, so long gone from your life
but never absent from your heart.

Then you cross Rainbow Bridge together...."

- Author unknown

8. Memorials

There are as many ways to honor the passing of a beloved pet, as each of our furry friends is uniquely special to us.

For instance, you and your family may wish to have your companion cremated and preserve their ashes in a special urn or sprinkle their ashes along their favorite walk, or across the lake where they loved to swim.

Perhaps you will want to have a special marker, photo bereavement, photo engraved Rainbow Bridge Poem, or wooden plaque created in honor of your passed friend, or you may wish to keep their memory close to you at all times by having a DNA remembrance pendant or bracelet designed.

As well, there are support groups, such as Rainbow Bridge, which is a grief support community, to help you and your family through this painful period of loss and grief.

Chapter 17: Rescue Organizations

When you are considering rescuing a specific breed of dog or puppy, the first place to start your search will be with your local breeders, shelters and rescue groups.

There are many breed specific rescue organizations in Canada, the USA, the United Kingdom and many other countries and the easiest way to find one closest to you is to go online and type in the breed name of the dog you want to rescue next to the name of the city where you live.

1. Shelters

Here you can expect to pay an adoption fee to cover the cost of spaying or neutering, but this will be only a small percentage of what you would pay a breeder, and you will be saving a life at the same time.

2. Online Resources

Sites such as Petango, Adopt A Pet and Pet Finder can be good places to begin your search. Each of these online resources is a central gathering site for hundreds and hundreds of local shelters, humane societies and rescue groups.

3. Canine Clubs and Breeders

Another place to search will be clubs or breeders in your local area. These groups may have rescue dogs available.

Chapter 18: Resources & References

The following resources and references are listed alphabetically within their specific category and include web addresses.

1. Poison Control

ASPCA Poison Control: www.aspca.org

Poisonous Plants Affecting Dogs - Cornell University, Department of Animal Science
www.ansi.cornell.edu/plants/dogs/

2. Breeders, Registries & Rescues

Adopt A Pet: www.adoptapet.com
Bull Terrier Club of America: www.btca.com
Credetta Bull Terriers: www.credettabullterriers.co.uk
Kenandai Bull Terriers: www.kendaibullterriers.com
National Dog Tattoo Register: www.dog-register.co.uk
National Dog Registry: www.nationaldogregistry.com
Petango: www.petango.com
Pet Finder: www.petfinder.com
Ragnarok Bull Terriers: www.ragnarokbullterriers.com
Reddirt Bull Terriers: www.reddirtbullterriers.com
The American Kennel Club: www.akc.org
The Bull Terrier Club: www.thebullterrierclub.org
The Kennel Club: www.thekennelclub.org.uk

3. Equipment, Supplies & Services

Andis Dog Clippers: www.andis.com
Dog Bowl for Your Dog: www.dogbowlforyourdog.com
Dremel™ Nail Grinder for Dogs: www.dremel.com
EduMal: www.edumal.tv
K-9 Super Heroes Dog Whispering:
www.k-9superheroesdogwhispering.com
Mim VarioCage: www.mightymitedoggear.com
Must Have Publishing: www.musthavepublishing.com

Modern Puppies: www.modernpuppies.com
Oster Dog Clippers: www.osterpro.com
Potty Patch: www.pottypatch.com
Poochie Bells™: www.poochie-pets.net
Remove Urine Odors: www.removeurineodors.com
Sleepy Pod: www.sleepypod.com
Springer Bicycle Jogger: available online
Tell Bell™: www.tellbell.com
Tick Twister: www.ticktwister.com
ThunderShirt: www.thundershirt.com
Wahl Dog Clippers: www.wahl.com

4. Memorials

Rainbow Bridge: www.rainbowbridge.com

Published by IMB Publishing 2015

Copyright and Trademarks: This publication is Copyrighted 2015 by IMB Publishing. All products, publications, software and services mentioned and recommended in this publication are protected by trademarks. In such instance, all trademarks & copyright belong to the respective owners. All rights reserved. No part of this book may be reproduced or transferred in any form or by any means, graphic, electronic, or mechanical, including photocopying, recording, taping, or by any information storage retrieval system, without the written permission of the authors. Pictures used in this book are either royalty free pictures bought from stock-photo websites or have the source mentioned underneath the picture.

Disclaimer and Legal Notice: This product is not legal or medical advice and should not be interpreted in that manner. You need to do your own due-diligence to determine if the content of this product is right for you. The authors and the affiliates of this product are not liable for any damages or losses associated with the content in this product. While every attempt has been made to verify the information shared in this publication, neither the author nor the affiliates assume any responsibility for errors, omissions or contrary interpretation of the subject matter herein. Any perceived slights to any specific person(s) or organization(s) are purely unintentional. We have no control over the nature, content and availability of the web sites listed in this book.

The inclusion of any web site links does not necessarily imply a recommendation or endorse the views expressed within them. IMB Publishing takes no responsibility for, and will not be liable for, the websites being temporarily unavailable or being removed from the Internet.

The accuracy and completeness of information provided herein and opinions stated herein are not guaranteed or warranted to produce any particular results, and the advice and strategies, contained herein may not be suitable for every individual. The author shall not be liable for any loss incurred as a consequence of the use and application, directly or indirectly, of any information presented in this work. This publication is designed to provide information in regard to the subject matter covered.

The information included in this book has been compiled to give an overview of the subject and detail some of the symptoms, treatments etc. that are available. It is not intended to give medical advice. For a firm diagnosis of any health condition, and for a treatment plan suitable for you and your dog, you should consult your veterinarian or consultant.

The writer of this book and the publisher are not responsible for any damages or negative consequences following any of the treatments or methods highlighted in this book. Website links are for informational purposes and should not be seen as a personal endorsement; the same applies to the products detailed in this book. The reader should also be aware that although the web links included were correct at the time of writing, they may become out of date in the future.

CPSIA information can be obtained
at www.ICGtesting.com
Printed in the USA
BVHW091101251120
594186BV00012B/987

Hydroponics for Beginners

A Step by Step Beginners Guide to Building Your Own Hydroponic Garden with Easy and Affordable Ways

Sam Cooper

© **Copyright 2018 by Sam Cooper - All rights reserved.**

The content contained within this book may not be reproduced, duplicated or transmitted without direct written permission from the author or the publisher.

Under no circumstances will any blame or legal responsibility be held against the publisher, or author, for any damages, reparation, or monetary loss due to the information contained within this book, either directly or indirectly.

Legal Notice:

This book is copyright protected. It is only for personal use. You cannot amend, distribute, sell, use, quote or paraphrase any part, or the content within this book, without the consent of the author or publisher.

Disclaimer Notice:

Please note the information contained within this document is for educational and entertainment purposes only. All effort has been executed to present accurate, up to date, reliable, complete information. No warranties of any kind are declared or implied. Readers acknowledge that the author is not engaged in the rendering of legal, financial, medical or professional advice.

The content within this book has been derived from various sources. Please consult a licensed professional before attempting any techniques outlined in this book.

By reading this document, the reader agrees that under no circumstances is the author responsible for any losses, direct or indirect, that are incurred as a result of the use of the information contained within this document, including, but not limited to, errors, omissions, or inaccuracies.

Table of Contents

- ❖ **Chapter 1**..6
  Hydroponics, what it is?

- ❖ **Chapter 2**..7
  The History of Hydroponics

- ❖ **Chapter 3**..11
  Advantages and Disadvantages

- ❖ **Chapter 4**..18
  Hydroponics or Aquaponics?

- ❖ **Chapter 5**..21
  The Equipment

- ❖ **Chapter 6**..72
  Hydroponics grow system

- ❖ **Chapter 7**..122

    Starting seeds

- ❖ **Chapter 8**..128

    Cloning

- ❖ **Chapter 9**..130

    Best plants for Hydroponics

- ❖ **Chapter 10**..137

    Nutrient Solution

- ❖ **Chapter 11**..164

    Monitoring

- ❖ **Chapter 12**..179

    Crop Health

❖ **Chapter 13** 185
<u>Most Commons Problems</u>

Conclusion..190

Chapter 1

Hydroponics, what it is?

For many decades' farmers have been growing the same crop in the same field. This leads to degradation of the soil, which results in produce that is less nutritious compared to a few decades ago.

In hydroponics, all the necessary nutrients are delivered by the nutrients dissolved in the water.

Hydroponics is an excellent option for growing your crops. Most of the time, the environment is controlled which reduces the risk of pests and diseases. Growing indoors or in a greenhouse will likely reduce the need for pesticides.

Hydroponics can produce crops faster than conventional methods. Produce can be located close to the consumer because these can be grown indoors without the need for soil.

Put simply; Hydroponics is a method of growing plants with water, a nutrient solution, and a growing medium. There is no soil involved. The word 'hydroponics' actually reflects this; 'hydro' means water and 'ponos' means labor.

Hydroponics is not a new approach to creating food; it is an ancient practice.

Let's explore where hydroponics made its first appearance.

Chapter 2

History

Let's go back in time and take a quick look at the history of hydroponics.

The hanging gardens of Babylon are perhaps one of the first examples of hydroponics in action. These gardens date from 600 BC. That is a long time ago!

King Nebuchadnezzar II built them during his forty-three-year reign to keep his wife happy as she was missing the plants and flowers of her homeland.

The plants were placed in growing media instead of soil.

The gardens are said to have been created as a series of terraces, all fed from a chain irrigation bucket system. Evidence of this type of structure was found both by a German archaeologist Robert Koldewey between 1899 and 1917.

It is an impressive achievement, and if it were real, it would have been a great example of early hydroponics.

Fast forward to the 11th century, and there is another excellent example of hydroponics in action. This design was created by the Aztecs, who had been driven off their land. They settled by Lake Tenochtitlan but were unable to grow crops on the marshland.

Instead, they built reed rafts and put some soil on top of them before floating them on the lake, allowing their crops to grow.

It should be noted that the lake was full of nutrients (nitrates) from the fish, which helped the crops to grow faster. This is similar to the principle of aquaponics.

Cultivating crops on reed rafts

The floating gardens in China were created in the 13th century, along with similar principles.

Despite these prominent examples, research and formal papers weren't created until the 17th century. A wave of research was started by the publication of Sir Francis Bacon's work in the 1620s.

By the end of the 17th century, John Woodward, an English scientist, was experimenting with plants grown in rainwater, river water, and water mixed with soil. His findings suggested that hydroponics speeds up the growth of plants and that plants grew better in less pure water, in essence, water that had a higher mineral content.

Modern research shows that his theory regarding 'less pure' water making plants grow stronger and faster was correct.

Effectively, the 'less pure' water had the nutrients the plants needed.

Fast forward to 1938, and you'll find a publication called, The water culture method for growing plants without soil, it was produced by two scientists, Dennis Hoagland, and Daniel Arnon.

This research is considered one of the most important texts about hydroponics. Some of the techniques are still used today, like the Kratky method and deep-water culture systems.

This research was used on Wake island in the pacific. Deepwater culture was used to successfully grow tomatoes, beans, and a host of other vegetables. It was the first time that hydroponics was done on a large scale, which proved that hydroponics was a viable option for feeding large amounts of people efficiently.

During the Second World War, several of these systems were adopted on small, otherwise barren, Pacific islands, helping to feed those involved in the war effort.

The second half of the 20th century saw considerable advancements in hydroponics availability thanks to plastic.

The ability to create plastic hydroponics tanks didn't just make it easier to grow plants commercially. It also made it possible for people to start building their DIY home systems.

The 1990s also saw experiments with growing plants using hydroponics in the desert and even as part of the space program. This was the real trigger for commercial production and even vertical farming ideas.

NASA's work, as part of the space program, was to help astronauts survive in space, or even on a different planet.

Hydroponics is a fantastic solution for delivering essential nutrients to astronauts on increasingly long space journeys.

Because the system doesn't need soil and uses minimal water, it's the perfect solution for growing food in space.

Of course, this will be the most expensive lettuce ever cultivated by humankind.

Perhaps the most important research nowadays, is the development of LED lighting systems, blue and red lights have been used to increase the growth of plants.

The research is also looking at the effect of different light colors and atmospheric pressure. Most of this research is published online. We can benefit from these studies for our hobby systems.

So, when you start your hydroponics system, spare a moment to consider all those that have gone before. You're in great company, but that doesn't mean to say there isn't room for improvement!

Advantages and Disadvantages

Any system of growing produce is going to have advantages and disadvantages. It is a good idea to be aware of what these are before you start your DIY system. We will begin by looking at the advantages.

The Advantages

Grow anywhere

There are large areas of the world that can't be used to grow food, specifically deserts and dry regions. But, providing you can get water to these places, you can set up a hydroponics system and grow crops.

Considering much of the space in a dessert is classified as 'useless,' that is a real bonus! It doesn't even matter what the soil is made of.

Fewer pests

Soil-borne pests often attack plants. Because soil is not an essential part of a hydroponics system, the risk of disease is reduced. It should be noted that it is not eliminated as air-borne pests can still introduce diseases to your hydroponics system.

Greenhouses or indoor growing setups act as a barrier for pests. One of the advantages of a greenhouse is that you can release beneficial insects that eat pests. If you are using a greenhouse, these beneficial insects are contained.

Faster growing time

Plants that are grown in hydroponics will grow more quickly because they have access to all the nutrients and trace elements. They provide more yield and are more pest resistant. In short, hydroponics gives better results than conventional farming methods.

Research shows that lettuce grown hydroponically can yield as much as eighty-eight pounds/ ten feet squared (forty-one kilograms/meter squared) a year. As opposed to just eight and a half pounds/ ten feet squared (three point nine kilograms/meter squared) a year when grown conventionally.

Water usage was ten times lower with hydroponics than soil-grown crops. Harvest was 11 times greater with hydroponics than soil.

These numbers seem to speak for themselves, but you have additional costs when doing hydroponics, which have to be factored in. In this study, they also calculated that the energy cost was 82 times greater in hydroponics than soil. This is very important to know for commercial operations.

Better Control

Hydroponics farming allows you to monitor and adjust the nutrients in the water. This gives you much more control over the growing environment, helping to produce the best possible yield in the shortest possible time.

Water Usage

Research concludes that hydroponics uses ninety percent less water than growing plants conventionally in the field. This is because the water is re-circulated most of the times, water is only lost through evaporation or a water exchange.

The Disadvantages

With the advantages, you will always have disadvantages. Let's look at them next.

High set-up costs

Hydroponics has higher start-up costs than soil-grown crops. This is because you need several items to start with:

- A water tank
- A pump to re-circulate the water
- A setup for your plants to grow (NFT, DWC) A grow medium
- The need to buy nutrients Sometimes artificial light sources

Airborne diseases

Although the risk of soil-based diseases is lower, airborne diseases can happen, and because of the nature of hydroponics, these diseases can quickly spread between plants because they are planted closer to each other.

It is essential to be aware of the main signs of plant disease and react a fast as possible.

Another example of a disease that is not airborne is Pythium (root rot), which can be introduced to a hydroponic system through the water and will result in browning of the roots.

Luckily, you can control most of these by proper design of the system, which we will talk about later in the book.

Knowledge

Understanding the principles behind hydroponics is relatively straightforward, although some learning is necessary. However, to properly run the system, you need to understand the different pieces of equipment involved and how to monitor and adjust nutrient levels.

Getting this right is essential to creating a long-lasting system, but it can be a steep learning curve. If you are not having success from the first time, see it as a learning experience and not as a defeat.

Monitoring

If you grow crops using conventional soil-based methods, you'll be able to leave your plants for several days. Nature has a habit of finding a way to help plants grow in almost any situation.

If you've created a hydroponics system, you should check for visible problems and check the nutrient levels quite often.

Having a mechanical failure can have an extremely negative effect on your hydroponics system, potentially killing your plants!

Of course, there are several ways to automate parts of the system, but this should not be your primary concern when you create your first hobby system.

Electricity

Electricity is essential to run the pumps, supply artificial light, heating or cooling, and air movement. All these additions will result in a higher electrical bill, which is an additional cost.

Water and electricity do not generally mix well, making this a safety risk that you need to be aware of.

If anything happens to the electricity supply, your plants can suffer surprisingly quickly. You should have a back-up option to run the pump for a few hours in a commercial system. This can be done with a solar setup or a backup generator.

Hydroponics vs. Aquaponics

You may have heard of aquaponics as an alternative to hydroponics. It works on a similar basis, but it isn't the same.

In hydroponics, plants grow in water, which is enriched with the right nutrients to encourage growth. These nutrients have to be added regularly.

This is why it is so important to check the pH, nutrient levels, and temperature regularly. Only by doing this will you be able to ensure you have the optimum environment for plant growth.

In hydroponics, you often need to do a partial water exchange. After that, you need to make sure the pH and nutrient levels are back at the advised level. An aquaponics system is, most of the time, a closed-loop with minimal water loss.

The significant difference between these two systems is that aquaponics has fish in the water. You will need to feed the fish, which will turn the protein-rich feed into ammonia. Bacteria will convert the ammonia into nitrates, which is food for the plants.

The fish provide 10 of the 13 nutrients the plant needs. The water is always returned to the fish tank.

This makes it more self-contained than hydroponics but needs more knowledge, making it more complicated than a hydroponic system.

You would need to supplement three nutrients to the aquaponics system, which are Iron, Potassium, and Calcium. The rest is supplied from the fish and fish food.

Aquaponics systems allow you to produce two sources of food from one system. The fish element makes the process fun and can help to attract customers if you are selling your products directly to customers or restaurants.

It is also essential to be aware that an aquaponics system needs to be cycled before you can start growing plants; this ensures the bacteria are present, which converts fish waste to plant nutrients. This means it will take longer to start growing plants with an aquaponics system than you can with a hydroponics system.

Aquaponics systems are also more expensive to establish.

For these reasons, hydroponics has become the more popular option for commercial farming, while aquaponics is the preferred option for small scale productions, backyard systems, or college demonstration systems.

Of course, there are plenty of people who will argue the case for either of these systems as both provide better yield, faster-growing crops, and less space than soil-based farming methods.

If you want to read a good book about aquaponics, I recommend reading the book written by Nick Brooke called Aquaponics for Beginners.

In the next chapter, we are starting our hydroponics journey by looking at what equipment we need to get started.

Equipment

Monitoring equipment

pH meter

pH is a measure of how acidic or how alkaline water is. A pH of 7 is neutral. pH levels that range from 1 to 6 are acidic, and levels from 8 to 14 are considered alkaline or basic.

Different plants have their preferences regarding pH levels. To ensure the best possible growth, you need to have a way of testing and then adjusting the pH level of your water.

For example:

Cabbage likes pH levels of 7.5 Tomatoes like a pH of 6-6.5 Sweet potatoes like a pH of 5.2-6 Peppers like a pH of 5.5-7

Lettuce and broccoli like a pH of 6-7

We will talk about why balancing pH is essential later in the book.

A pH meter can be obtained from local hydroponics stores or online. You need to calibrate the sensor with the calibration powder that comes with the meter. A basic pH meter will cost you $10 to $20.

A basic pH meter

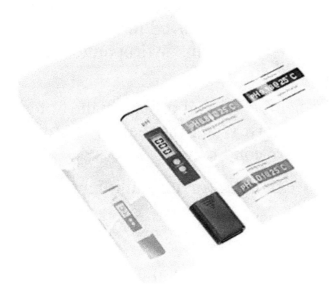

Don't use paper test strips for the water because they are inaccurate. Most of the time, a pH meter is offered in combination with a TDS or EC meter, which we will talk about next.

EC meter

Electrical conductivity is a measurement of how easily electricity passes through the water, the higher the ion content, the better it is at conducting electricity.

All water has ions in it. When you add nutrients to the water, you are increasing the ion content, effectively increasing the electrical conductivity.

EC or Electrical Conductivity is an integral part of the hydroponics equation. The simplest way of explaining this is as a guide to salts dissolved in water. Its unit is siemens per meter, but in hydroponics, we use millisiemens per meter.

In short, the higher the number of salts in the water, the higher the conductivity. Water that has no salt (distilled water) will have zero conductivity.

Lettuce likes an EC of 1.2 (or 1.2 millisiemens), while basil likes an EC of 2.

That is why it is so important to know your EC and what your plants prefer, it will help you to ensure your system is at the right level.

However, electrical conductivity needs are also affected by the weather. When it is hot, the plants evaporate more water. That is why you need to decrease the EC in hot summer months. In colder winter months, you need to increase the EC.

In warm weather, you need to decrease the EC. In cold weather, you need to increase the EC.

An EC meter doesn't tell you the specific amount of which mineral or fertilizer is in the water. If you only use a nutrient solution using the right ratios, you shouldn't worry.

Just because it doesn't monitor individual nutrients, doesn't mean it's not useful. Salt levels that are too high will damage your plants.

You generally need to keep them between 0.8 and 1.2 for leafy greens and between 2 and 3.5 for fruiting crops like tomatoes. The source of the water can influence the EC reading. More on this later.

Sometimes, you see the recommended nutrient levels listed as CF. CF is the conductivity factor. This is like EC, used in Europe. If you multiply EC by ten, you will become CF.

For example, lettuce grows best in an EC of 0.8 to 1.2. This is a CF of 8 to 12.

TDS meter

TDS stands for total dissolved salts. You may hear some hydroponics growers referring to the TDS and not EC. These are both used to determine the strength of your hydroponic solution. If you buy a TDS meter, there will also be an option to switch to EC readings.

It is crucial to understand that TDS is a calculated figure. TDS readings are converted from an EC reading. The problem occurs when you don't know which calculation method was used to produce the TDS; there are several different ones.

In general, EC and CF readings are used in Europe, while TDS is an American measurement. But, regardless of which measurement you choose to use, they are both effectively the same thing: a measure of the nutrient levels in your solution.

The NaCl Conversion factor

This is effectively measuring salt in the water. The conversion factor for this mineral is your micro siemens figure multiplied by any number between 0.47 and 0.5. You'll find most TDS meters use 0.5. This is the easiest one for you to remember and calculate. Most of the meters sold will use the NaCl conversion factor.

As an example, if you have a reading of 1 EC (1 milli Siemens or 1000 micro Siemens), you will have a TDS reading of 500ppm.

Natural Water Conversion factor

This conversion factor is referred to as the 4-4-2; this quantifies its contents. Forty percent sodium sulfate, forty percent sodium bicarbonate, and twenty percent sodium chloride.

Again, the conversion factor is a range, this time between 0.65 and

0.85. Most TDS meters will use 0.7.

For example, 1 EC (1000 micro Siemens) will be 700 ppm with a TDS meter that uses the natural water conversion.

Potassium Chloride, KCl Conversion factor

This conversion factor is not a range this time. It is simply a figure of

0.55. Your EC meter reading 1EC or 1000 micro Siemens will equate to 550 ppm.

These are not all the possible conversion options, but they are the most common. The first, NaCl is the most used today.

Dissolved oxygen sensor

Plant roots need oxygen to remain healthy and ensure the plant grows properly. The dissolved oxygen sensor will help you to understand how much oxygen is available in the water and ensure it's enough to keep your plants healthy.

If plants don't get enough oxygen to their roots, they can die. A minimum of 5 ppm is recommended.

A dissolved oxygen meter will be expensive for the hobbyist to buy, especially when you are starting. That is why dissolved oxygen meters are generally not purchased by people who do hydroponics for fun.

A good meter can cost you $170 to $500 for a reputable brand.

You do not need to invest in one if you oxygenate the water. Oxygenation of the water can be done by using an air pump with an airstone in the water tank. Depending on the method of growing, you don't need to aerate the water.

The dissolved oxygen in the water will be at its lowest during the summer. The water heats up, and the dissolved oxygen becomes less available. While your plants can do very well in winter, they might lack oxygen during summer.

Net Pots

In some systems, you are going to need net pots to hold the plants. This is mostly true for deep water culture (DWC), Kratky, wick systems, Aeroponics, fogponics, dutch buckets, and possibly vertical towers.

Make sure you get the net pots with a lip on top to keep them from falling through. The standard size for lettuce is two inches (five centimeters).

If you want to use tomatoes with dutch buckets, six inches (fifteen centimeters) is recommended.

If you are creating a new system on a budget, there are a variety of other options that can be used instead of buying net pots. For example, plastic cups with lots of holes in them, or simply fine netting on a wireframe. Use your imagination!

Humidity and temperature sensor

Estimating temperatures and humidity levels will lead to mistakes. I recommend getting a simple humidity and temperature sensor, so you don't need to guess. Most of them will cost you no more than $15.

Germination tray and dome

You need to start seeds in a dedicated germination tray. Most of these trays are 10x10 or 10x20 inches (25x25 or 25x50 centimeters) and generally include a humidity dome.

These trays are used to let your seeds germinate and keep the humidity high. After the first true leaves appear, it is time to transplant them into your system. Usually, this is after ten to fifteen days.

The humidity should be between sixty and seventy percent, while temperatures should be 68-77°F or 20-25°C.

Seed starter cubes

If you are growing plants from seed, you can't simply place seeds in the net pots. They'll get washed away or sink. Instead, you need a seed starter cube. These cubes provide a place for the seed to start growing roots and flourish, safely.

Several materials can be used as your grow media when starting seeds:

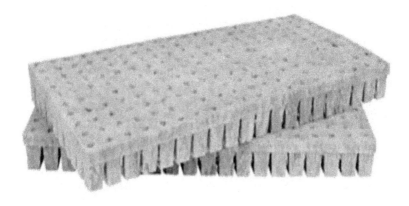

Rockwool cubes

These are made from a combination of basalt and chalk, spun together. The result is a small cube that is similar in consistency to cotton candy. Your seeds can be placed into the Rockwool cube where they will start to germinate.

The cube goes in the net pot and your seed should have everything it needs to start growing. Providing it has access to the nutrient-rich water. These cubes come in all shapes and sizes.

Generally, you would only need a small one or one and a half inch or cube. Depending on the method of growing, you need to add some grow media to support the cube and block sunlight from creating algae on the cube.

Two seed starting cubes sheets

You can separate each cube from the bigger sheet. I recommend using gloves for this because the Rockwool can be irritating on the skin.

As with every seed starter cube, you must soak it in pH neutral water of six before using it. This ensures that the seed has better germination rates.

Coco Coir

An alternative to Rockwool cubes is coco coir. This is simply the fibrous coat of a coconut.

Coco coir is an organic media which will break down over time. Some people use it because it is environmentally friendly and renewable. I don't recommend it to start with. It can break down and clog your system if you are not careful.

It can begin to rot somewhere, and before you know it, make your water quality terrible.

Oasis cubes

Another seed-starting cube is the oasis cube. They retain moisture well and are very soft. This makes it easy for the roots to penetrate the medium but also makes them brittle. Oasis cubes are also used as a growing media. These cubes are very popular with NFT systems.

Sponges

Sponges are used most of the time as a cheap alternative to Rockwool or oasis cubes. However, they do not absorb or retain moisture that well. That is why using sponges is not a carefree method of seed starting. They are not as environmentally friendly as the other seed starting cubes.

Growing media

After you have placed your seed in the seed starter cubes and they have started to germinate, you will see roots coming out of the starter cube.

This is the time for you to start transplanting them into their second grow space.

The grow media will depend on which growing technique you are going to use.

For floating rafts and NFT, you do not need any growing media. For other methods like the Kratky, dutch buckets, or wick system, you may need to add some growing media.

The use of grow media also depends on how big the plant is going to be. Lettuce doesn't need growing media because it doesn't need the support. Tomatoes need growing media to support the plant.

Growing media gives your plant stability and space for the roots to further develop.

Hydroton

This is the most popular growing media.

Hydroton is created from clay that has been heated to high temperatures. The result is a very porous material that is made into small balls.

Hydroton is very lightweight, ensuring your pots aren't under any undue stress. It is excellent to keep your seed starter cubes in place. It's also easy on the hands.

You should wash hydroton before using it to remove clay dust.

You can also re-sterilize this grow media, but it can be time- consuming, especially if you have a lot of it.

Sterilizing or re-sterilizing is vital as your grow media can have bacteria or other micro-organisms that could be harmful to your plants. Whether using it for the first time or re-using the growing media, cleaning alone may not be enough to get rid of these bacteria. You need to sterilize the growing media to ensure it is safe for re-use.

Sterilizing involves using either heat or a chemical to kill all organisms on the growing media. A popular chemical choice is hydrogen peroxide.

You will need a thirty-five percent hydrogen peroxide solution and then wash the clay balls in it thoroughly. Mix one part of hydrogen peroxide (thirty-five percent) with eleven parts of water. This will lower it to a three percent solution.

Most importantly, you need to rinse the growing media several times to ensure all traces of the hydrogen peroxide are gone.

You could also use a ten percent bleach solution. A bleach solution is used for sterilizing NFT troughs or other equipment in your system as well.

The alternative is to heat the growing media in an oven with a temperature of 180°F (82°C) or more, for at least thirty minutes.

It will pasteurize and remove fungal type microorganisms. To get rid of all organisms, you need to sterilize which involves at least thirty minutes at 212°F (100°C).

Warning: Doing this in your kitchen will leave a sour odor that lingers.

Perlite

When you take minerals and expose them to extreme heat, you will force them to expand and pop like popcorn, effectively creating Perlite. This is another growing media that is pH neutral and extremely light. It's not good at retaining moisture.

Perlite is used by gardeners in their soil to increase aeration to the roots. It is excellent for dutch buckets (drip), wicking systems, or the Kratky method. More on these later.

You can get Perlite at any garden store, but you must be careful not to get it in your eyes.

When handling perlite, use a dust mask. The dust created when handling perlite is not healthy to breathe in.

Vermiculite

This silicon-based substance is exposed to the same high temperatures for forming Perlite. It also expands and is very similar to Perlite, and it is also pH neutral. The main difference is that Vermiculite is high in cation-exchange.

In simple terms, it is better at holding onto water and nutrition for release into the plant later. Vermiculite is too good at retaining moisture that it can suffocate the roots. That's why it's popular in a fifty/fifty mix with perlite.

Rockwool

As already described, Rockwool is an excellent choice for seed starting. The larger Rockwool cubes that range from three to six inches (seven to fifteen centimeters) can be used for an entire plant. It is pH neutral and easy to use. Rockwool is very good at wicking up the water.

Big Rockwool cubes

The big Rockwool cubes are mostly used for plants that have a long- life cycle. It is not financially viable to plant lettuce in these bigger grow blocks. The holes in these blocks are too big for seedlings. You need to use a Rockwool starter cube to grow your seedlings, and then move the plant with the starter cube into these bigger cubes.

Another method of growing is using Rockwool slabs. They are widely used in tomato farms. They are the largest Rockwool media you can find. You can fit several big rock wool cubes in one slab. One slab is a few feet long and comes in different sizes. You need to pre-soak these too.

Do not remove the plastic cover from these. The plastic keeps the moisture in and the light out. Drainage holes should be made at the bottom of the slab. Drip emitters should be inserted into the big Rockwool cubes.

Growstones

Growstones are made from recycled glass, which may seem like an unusual material for a hydroponics system.

Growstones are good for aeration and moisture retention. The fact that they can wick water up to four inches (ten centimeters) above the waterline means your plants will always have the water they need.

You shouldn't let the term glass put you off, they look like sharp edges, but they are not.

River rock

As the name suggests, this type of grow material comes from a riverbed. The rocks are naturally rounded off as the water removes the sharp edges. The irregular shapes of river rock means that there are plenty of air pockets, which makes it easier for the roots to become established.

If you are operating a flood and drain style hydroponics system, this can be the right choice.

But, if you need more water retention, river rock might not be the best option out there.

If you are on a tight budget and hydroton is a bit too expensive, river rock will be the best alternative. Use three-quarter inch (two centimeters) river rock for the best results.

River rock must be washed before you use it to ensure it is clean. If you are thinking of using this, it is worth noting that it is cumbersome, potentially preventing you from moving your system in the future.

Pine Shavings

This is not the same as sawdust, which will absorb water and block up your system. Pine shavings must be made from kiln-dried wood, and there must be no chemical fungicides in it. Your best bet for purchasing this inexpensive grow media is pet stores or a nearby wood processing factory.

The larger the shavings, the better the air pockets between them, which is good for the roots of your plants. Pine shavings are organic, so it will break down over time, making this a single-use growing media.

Water Absorbing Crystals

You may have heard of these as they are used in diapers and many other products. They are not a common addition to hydroponics systems yet.

They are also known as hydrogels or super absorbent polymer.

They expand and hold a large amount of water, which can then be slowly absorbed by the plants. These crystals will reduce or even eliminate air pockets. That means your roots won't get enough oxygen.

To overcome this, you'll need to mix the water-absorbing crystals fifty/fifty with river rock or hydroton. This will create the water and oxygen retention your plants need.

A one-pound bag will cost about $15. Search for 'Super Absorbent Hydro Gel Granules' or 'water storing crystals' online.

Make sure to get the pearls instead of the powder. The powder will make a mess. The size of the polymer will increase once it has been hydrated.

Account for the increase in size before transplanting. They are not a popular choice with hydroponics because of the price. They are only used with premium crops.

Pump

The pump is an essential part of almost all hydroponics systems. It is this that is responsible for moving the water around the system, ensuring the plants have the water and nutrients they need.

While you will learn later in the book of some systems that don't use a pump, the majority of hydroponics systems do.

The size of the pump will depend on the required flow rate and the head height of the pump.

We are going to look at head height first.

What is the head height of a pump?

Let's say you bought a two hundred and fifty gallons per hour pump. The pump tells you it is two hundred and fifty gallons per hour, so it should pump two hundred and fifty gallons per hour, right?

Not exactly,

You see, the flow rate of a pump is described with zero feet of head height (elevation). This means the pump will deliver two hundred and fifty gallons per hour without lifting it to your system. The flow rate will decrease once you start pumping the water up.

Determining head height

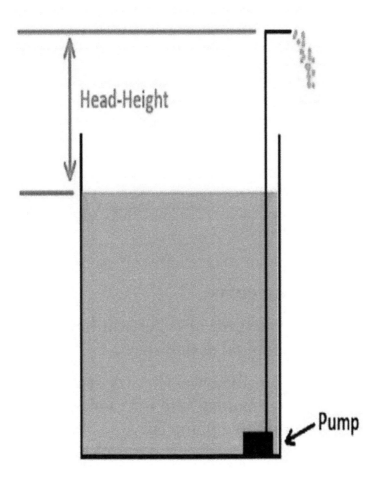

Luckily there are charts available for a pump that will indicate flow rate with a certain amount of head height. In the following image, you can see such a curve which is called 'a pump curve.' This curve puts the relation between flow rate and head height in a nice graph.

Six pumps combined in one graph

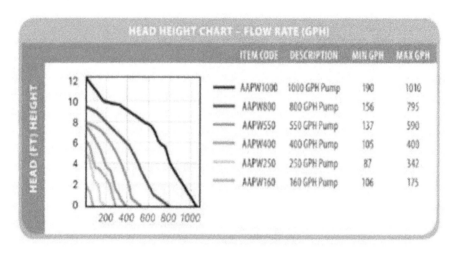

Reading the pump curve

Every decent manufacturer or seller will have a pump curve in their user manual or datasheet.

If you can't find it on their website, try searching for: 'name of pump + user manual' and with a bit of luck, you should see a pdf file with a pump curve.

Once you have found the pump curve of the pump you want to use, you need to look at the left axis first. Find the head height you have figured out for your system and draw a line to the right. Next, look for your required minimum flow rate and draw a vertical line. The point where these lines cross is your pump 'working' point.

If your working point is between two pump lines, you need to move up to the right. Never go to the left because you won't make it to the recommended minimum flow rate.

You need a pump of 400 gallons/hour (1500 liters/hour)

Let's imagine you need to pump two hundred and fifty gallons per hour. The elevation is three feet. Draw a line on the graph from your head height to the desired flow rate. The point where the two lines cross will be your desired pump flow rate.

If you would have taken the two hundred and fifty gallons per hour pump, it wouldn't make it to two hundred and fifty gallons per hour. It would be pumping one hundred and eighty gallons per hour.

Instead, you choose the four hundred gallons per hour pump if you want to pump at least two hundred and fifty gallons per hour with a head height of three feet.

The simplest rule to remember when purchasing a water pump is that you can use a split-flow back to the water reservoir to get the right water flow.

You can't increase the flow of your pump if it's not powerful enough. In other words, always purchase a pump that is more powerful than you need.

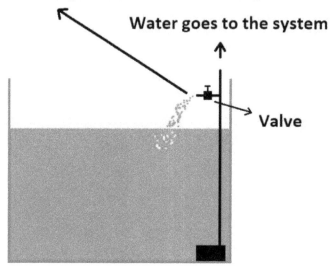

Split flow after the pump

Let's look at the water requirements for different systems.

Ebb and Flow or Flood and Drain

With the ebb and flow technique, you are flooding a container and draining it afterward. The size of the pump will depend on how big the volume of the container is and the height you need to pump it. As a rule of thumb, the time it takes for the water to flood the tray is five minutes.

Example: a flood tray that measures 2x2x1 ft, has a square footage of 4ft². We are going to flood the tray to 0.5ft in height. Multiply **(4ftx4ft) x 0.5 ft= (4ft³)**

Convert 2ft³ to gallons:

$2ft^3 \times 7.5 = 15$ gallons

It will take a fifteen gallon per hour pump one hour to fill the flood tray. But the rule of thumb said you need to flood the tray in five minutes.

$$\frac{60 \text{ minutes}}{5 \text{ minutes}} = 12$$

15 gallons x 12 = 180 gallons/hour

You need a 180 gallons per hour pump to fill the growing container in five minutes. Keep in mind that this is without head height. You need to determine the head height and choose a pump that will deliver 180 gallons per hour.

Flooding frequency depends on the growing media. Rockwool can be flooded once a day, while hydroton needs several cycles a day. This is because Rockwool can hold on to water longer than hydroton.

DWC (Floating rafts)

You do not need a water pump for floating rafts. If you are using a nutrient mixing tank, you should have one to pump the water from the tank to the floating raft troughs. You only need air stones under the rafts to provide oxygen to the roots.

Drip, Dutch buckets, NFT, and vertical systems

If you are using this kind of system, you are going to use drip irrigation. The diameter of these drip lines is small, thus does not need a high flow. One drip line of 3/8 inches (0.9cm) delivers eight gallons (thirty liters) per hour. You need to calculate how many drip lines your system needs.

Example: An NFT system needs one drip line in one gully to have the recommended flow rate of 0.5 liters per minute or ½ quart per minute. A system that has 20 gullies needs a pump with a minimum of:

```
(0.5 liters x 60 minutes)x20 gullies = 600 liters/hour
```

Convert liters to gallons:

$$\frac{600 \text{ liters}}{3.78} = 159 \text{ gallons per hour}$$

Again, without considering head height.

Aeroponics

If you are doing aeroponics, you need a high-pressure diaphragm pump. Aeroponics is for the advanced grower because it uses more technology than the general growing techniques. Your pump needs to have at least 80psi (5.5bar) depending on the nozzles you are using. The flow rate will depend on the nozzles too.

In many systems, the pump will not run continuously. The pump will run for a few minutes, which is regulated with a timer.

The Timer

The timer is a small part and yet a vital piece of any hydroponics system. Its role is to tell your pump or lights when to turn on and off.

It is important to note that the timer is not essential for every hydroponics system. NFT systems don't generally need a timer. Dutch bucket, drip systems, and flood and drain systems typically do.

You can program the timer to whatever time you want to get the pump or lights working. You can get mechanical and electronic timers. The mechanical ones are cheaper and can be set in thirty- minute intervals, great for lights but not for pumps. Mechanical timers will cost you around seven dollars apiece.

For pumps, you need the electronically regulated timers. They have a display and have intervals of one second or one minute. Electronically regulated timer will cost you around fifteen dollars apiece.

Electronic timer

Always read the rated power for every timer. It is not going to work if your devices are using a combined two thousand watts while the timer is rated for only fifteen hundred watts.

Fogger

You won't be surprised to find out that a fogger is a device that creates fog.

If you are planning on establishing a fogponics cloning system, you'll need one. The fogger is also known as a misting device. It vibrates two million times per second to turn the nutrient-rich water into a fog. This is then absorbed by your plants, giving them the nutrition they need. The fogger floats on the water surface using a floating device.

If you are using a fogger, you generally need a large body of water or exchange the water often. This is because the vibrations will heat the water. Plants, especially clones, do not like warm water.

Aeration pump

An aeration pump adds oxygen to your water. You may wonder why this is necessary as plants use carbon dioxide.

However, carbon dioxide is an essential part of the photosynthesis process, where energy is created for the plant.

Inadequate oxygen levels will prevent the plant from undertaking the fundamental processes that keep it alive. If you are growing plants in soil, you generally never have to think about oxygen levels.

But, in a hydroponics system, when the roots are submerged most of the time, you need to make sure they get enough oxygen for their needs.

The exact rate of dissolved oxygen (DO) will change depending on what plant you are growing and what the temperature of your water is. Most plants will do with 5ppm of dissolved oxygen. Lettuce requires a minimum of 4ppm. Crop failure happens at levels lower than 3ppm.

We talked about this earlier when looking at the dissolved oxygen sensor.

The pump disturbs the water surface, which is creating movement. This movement enables the water to absorb more oxygen.

It should be noted that your air pump must use fresh air. If it is inside your grow room, there is a good possibility that it will be sending carbon dioxide-rich air into your system, which will not offer the same benefits as air from outside.

If the temperature of the water increases, dissolved oxygen will decrease. You have to make sure dissolved oxygen is always above the minimum recommended ppm.

If you have root rot, you need to increase the aeration of the water. Dissolved oxygen increases root growth, which will lead to more prominent root structures.

The roots of a successful hydroponics system are very different than roots that do not get enough oxygen. Roots that get a lot of oxygen look white and have fine root hairs. Roots without much exposure to air are thicker and have less root hairs.

Heat mat

Your seedlings might require a heat mat if it's colder. This is to help them germinate better. Set the heat mat at a temperature of 68°F (25°C), any higher than 77°F (25°C) will be counterproductive for germination.

Heat mat from Vivosun with build-in thermostat

Root conditioner

A root conditioner helps young seedlings to develop their roots. This is optional, but if you have problems with slow growth, give it a try. Most of the time this is an organic brown liquid like root hume from simple grow solutions.

Dose for simple grow root hume solution:

One capful in one liter of water or ¼ gallon.

Instead of soaking your seed starter cubes in a half-strength nutrient solution, you are going to add the root conditioner too.

Seeds

You need seeds to grow plants. It is better to use seeds; then it is to buy the seedling from a distributor. It will have dirt on the roots, and you need to wash it off before transplanting it into your system.

Using seeds will take longer but will limit the risk of soil born diseases.

If you are using small seeds, consider getting pelleted seeds. Pelleted seeds are seeds that are coated in clay or another substance to make it easier at handling.

Grow lights

Depending on where you are placing your setup, you may decide that your plants will benefit from some extra light.

Grow lights are the best way to do this because they have the light spectrum that the plants like. The lights you get in a hardware store are designed for households and probably won't give you the desired intensity (lumens) or light spectrum (Kelvin or PAR).

Light spectrum

If you go shopping for a fluorescent tube grow light you will have two choices. Buying cool blue lights (6500K) or warm red lights (4000K).

For seedlings and vegetative growth, it is best to use the cold blue light. Plants use this light to create energy to grow. Use these for leafy crops like lettuce, kale, basil, etc.

The other light spectrum is warm red light. This is used for growing fruiting crops like strawberries, tomatoes, etc. The red light will make sure the fruit the plant produces is big.

If the plant lacks the red spectrum, the produced fruits will be smaller.

Professional growers use a combination of these two. They usually start with a clone from a mature plant and put it under a blue light. The blue light spectrum will encourage growth and leaf development.

Once the plant reaches the desired foliage and produces signs of fruiting, they switch to a red color spectrum. The red color spectrum is used to develop bigger fruits.

The recent rise in the cultivation of medicinal plants will use the same technique. Instead of developing fruits, they create bigger flowers with red lights.

If you use red light from the beginning, your plant will stretch and grow tall. Most of the time, this is not desirable.

These are the goals of each growing stage:

1. Seedling:
    - Root growth
    - Foliage growth

2. Vegetative stage:
    - Root growth
    - Foliage growth

Stem growth

3. Flowering stage:
    - Creation of fruits
    - flowers

We need to adapt our light spectrum to each of these growing stages. The light spectrum is also called color temperature. Light spectrum or kelvin is not to be confused with PAR.

Light intensity

The intensity of light is also important. The higher the intensity of the light, the more energy it provides to the plant. The unit of light intensity is lumens.

The higher the intensity of the grow light, the farther away you need to suspend it from the plant (less lux), which will cover more growing area.

Some grow lights like the expensive LED lights can decrease light intensity for a particular PAR light spectrum. This is used to switch between one of the three stages mentioned before.

Lux is often confused with light intensity (lumens). They say that one lumen is one lux, which is not true. One lux is one lumen per square meter.

Let's explain it with an example.

A light bulb has 1000 lumens. If I were to measure the lumens with a lux meter, I would get different readings when I hold it closer or further away. The further away the lux meter is measuring, the lower the lux that is measured.

If we use the light bulb of 1000 lumens and concentrate it into an area of ten square feet (one square meter), we would get 1000 lux. If we were to spread the light over one hundred and seven square feet (ten square meters), we would have 100lux.

Thus, $1 \text{ Lux} = 1 \text{ lumen}/m^2$

PAR

PAR or Photosynthetic active radiation is the light that plants absorb in their different spectrums. PAR light is used for photosynthesis of the plant. While the light spectrum (Kelvin) describes the light to the human eye, PAR gives you the type of light each plant uses. PAR is more accurate for growing plants than the light spectrum (Kelvin) because it's the spectrum that the plant sees.

PAR is shown in a wavelength that is in nanometers (nm).

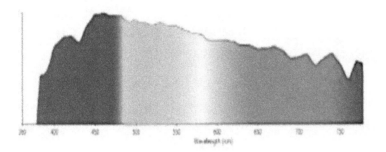

It reaches from 400 nanometers, which is blue to 700 nanometers, which is red.

Designers for office spaces and residential buildings use Kelvin while farmers use PAR. Some grow lights like T5 fluorescents use the Kelvin scale to indicate light spectrum.

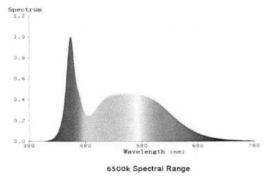

We can see from the previous image that blue fluorescent lights are not only blue but contains other colors that are not visible for the human eye.

Light duration (photoperiod)

The light duration depends on the plant itself. Different plants have different needs for light duration. Lettuce, for example, has a recommended minimum light duration of twelve hours a day.

This means, to optimally grow lettuce, you should expose it to light for at least twelve hours each day.

The light duration during the life cycle of a plant can change. For example, the light duration where tomatoes are in their vegetative stage will be different than their fruiting stage.

PPF

PPF is a measurement of how many photons of light per second hits your plants. PPF is called Photosynthetic Photon Flux. Its unit is umol/s or micromol per second.

When people measure PAR under their plant canopy, they are referring to PPF. Throughout time, these terms are used interchangeably

PPFD

PPFD or photosynthetic Photon Flux Density is the measurement of Photosynthetic Photon Flux (PPF) per area. PPFD is expressed in $umol/s/m^2$ or micromol per second per square meter.

PFD

PFD or Photon flux density is the same as the PPFD but with ultraviolet and far-red colors, which are out of the standard 400nm to 700nm PAR spectrum.

New research indicates that the wavelengths that are considered not usable to a plant are indeed usable to plants. But these are out of the PAR range of 400 to 700nm. That's why the first P has been removed. The first P stands for photosynthetic.

PFD takes to whole spectrum into consideration instead of only the PPFD. PFD is not used that much yet.

DLI

The DLI or daily light integral is the amount of light a plant receives in one day per square meter. DLI is the PPFD per day. The unit of DLI is micromol per square meter per day, or simply umol/m²/day. DLI is the amount of sunlight or artificial light a surface receives each day.

Each plant has a recommended DLI. If you are growing outdoors or in a greenhouse, you can look at a map that displays the DLI in different parts of the USA.

You need to have a light source (sun or artificial) that delivers the daily amount of DLI to the plant in their specific light duration. Any DLI that is over the recommended DLI would be a waste of energy because plants have light saturation.

Light saturation is the point where plants are no longer able to do photosynthesis. This means that plants can't absorb more light per day or given time frame (usually twenty-four hours).

Recommended DLI values:

Leafy greens: 10-25 mol/m²/day

Flowering crops: 25-35 mol/m²/day

To make sure your plant receives enough DLI, we are going to calculate DLI with an example.

Calculating DLI

You need to calculate your DLI to get the most efficient power usage for the most crop growth. I'm going to use lettuce with T5 fluorescents as an example to grow lettuce in one square meter.

Lettuce likes a DLI of 12-14 mol/m²/day. Next, we need to know how many lumens our grow light has. You can find this in the datasheet of the light. The one I'm using has 5000 lumens per four feet T5 tube.

Next, we will convert the lumens to PPF (Photosynthetic Photon Flux), which will give us umol/s (micro mols per second). I do this by using the following calculator:

I select the light color, which is cool blue or daylight (6500K), and insert the lumens that one 4ft T5 light will emit.

Conversion from lumens to PPF

Convert PPF to PPFD

Since we have a PPF of 115umol/s and we have a growing area of m² we do not need to convert it to PPFD. This is because PPFD is per square meter.

If we were to use these lights for two square meters, we would have to divide by two.

Thus,

115 umol/s = 115 umol/s/m²

PPFD to DLI

Next, we calculate PPFD (umol/s/m²) to DLI (mol). This is the formula to calculate the DLI:

$$\frac{\text{PPFD} \times 3600 \times \text{photoperiod in hours}}{1{,}000{,}000}$$

$$\frac{115 \times 3600 \text{ seconds} \times 12 \text{ hours}}{1{,}000{,}000} = 4.968 \text{ mol per m}^2 \text{ per day}$$

4.968 mol/m²/day is not enough for lettuce to grow efficiently.

We need a DLI of, at least, twelve for the lettuce to grow well. If I use more lights, I will get to the recommended DLI of twelve. I multiply the DLI by three because I am deciding to use three T5 light tubes. Then we become 14.9 mol/m²/day (3*4.968).

A DLI of 14.9 is slightly too high, which will result in wasted energy. Now we have two options:

- Increase the light duration
- Decrease the amount of T5 tubes

In this case, I chose to decrease the amount of T5 tubes and use two because it is cheaper just to buy two instead of three lights and increase the light duration slightly.

We calculate the DLI again,

$$\frac{(115 \times 2 \text{ lights}) \times 3600 \times 14.5 \text{ hours}}{1{,}000{,}000}$$

$$= 12 \text{ mol per m}^2 \text{ per day}$$

The final setup would be to use two 4ft T5 tubes per square meter to grow lettuce at a light interval of fourteen and a half hours every twenty-four hours.

The T5 light uses fifty-four watts per tube. Total running cost of this setup would be:

```
54 watts x 2 = 108 watts
```

```
14.5 hours x 108 watts = 1566 watt hours per day
```

Convert to Kilowatts:

$$\frac{1566 \text{ watt hours}}{1000} = 1.566 \text{ Kilowatt hour per day}$$

The national average is $0.12/kwh. Calculate cost per day:

1.566 x $0.12 = $0.187 per day

Calculate cost per year:

$0.187 x 365 = $68.5 per year

If we decided to use three lights and decrease the light interval, we would have a similar electricity cost. I choose to buy only two T5 tube fixtures because two are cheaper than three. The light tube itself is more affordable to replace (has an average of twenty thousand hours lifespan= four years running at fourteen and a half hours a day).

In greenhouses, you already have sunlight. This could be enough for the type of plant that you are growing in the summer. But if you want to grow crops during winter, you probably need to supplement light using light fixtures.

Photosynthesis

Photosynthesis is the process that creates energy for the plant. It happens inside the plant and needs carbon dioxide, water, and light.

It is something that only plants, algae, and some bacteria do. They take energy from the sun and turn it into chemical energy. The light energy transfers electrons from water to carbon dioxide, making carbohydrates for the plants to use as energy to grow.

A by-product of this process is oxygen because the carbon dioxide is used in the energy transfer process while the water is oxidized.

Perhaps the most significant thing about this is not the chemical process that plants do all the time but the fact that plants boost the amount of oxygen in the atmosphere.

Now you can see why plants and trees are so essential to the planet. They help to create an atmosphere that humans can live in. Another takeaway we see and know from studies is that increasing the levels of carbon dioxide in the air will accelerate the growth of a plant. It will also reduce the need for water and be more drought resistant.

If your plant has limited or no access to sunlight, it is going to need a light that provides a similar light spectrum to the sun.

While any light can be used to help your plant grow, you will probably want to choose one of the options below to get the best possible results.

Fluorescents (T5,8 and 12)

You are already familiar with fluorescents. It is not commonly used in houses anymore. In commercial and hobby systems, they are used to start seeds. This type of light puts out ten percent of their energy as light and the other ninety percent as heat. That is why you can place LED lights closer to your canopy than fluorescents.

T5 is the newest most efficient fluorescent on the market. T8 and T12 are less efficient but are cheaper to purchase. T5 is an excellent choice for growing vegetating plants inside. Make sure you use a reflector; it will reflect the light back to the plants.

4 T5 fluorescent in one fixture with a reflector

Fluorescents are used to grow microgreens and different vegetative plants. They have the right color spectrum (6500K white light) to grow them. Color spectrums of 3000K are also available. The fluorescents should be one foot (0.30 meters) above your plants and should be moved upwards if the plants are growing.

The T5 is the preferred choice as it's the most economical of the fluorescent tubes. They come in different fixtures and are supplied with a reflector and a daisy chain to adjust the height. They are great for starters who want to grow vegetative plants.

They are great for starting seedlings too.

HID

High-Intensity Discharge lights are commonly used in commercial hydroponic systems. They are, as their name suggests, extremely powerful (high light intensity). They need an electronic ballast, which is used for starting of the light.

They create an electric arc between two electrodes in a sealed chamber filled with a gas that emits the color stated on the bulb. Most bulbs have an E40 socket.

HID lights can be split into two subcategories:

- Metal Halide (MH)
  - Ceramic Metal Halide (CMH)
- High-Pressure Sodium (HPS)

MH

Metal Halide or MH is the best approach for growing vegetative plants like leafy greens on a big scale. The most common power ratings are:

-400W

-600W

-1000W

If you are growing flowering plants, you will want to use MH for the growing stage (foliage) and HPS for the flowering stage. You will need to get a lamp that accepts conversion bulbs to allow you to switch bulbs at the right stage. This way, you would only have to buy one fixture. Don't touch the bulbs with your hands, instead use a cloth or towel to handle them. The oil on your hands can damage the light and decrease its lifespan.

CMH

CMH or Ceramic metal halide or ceramic discharge metal halide is another type of metal halide lamp, which is ten to twenty percent more efficient than the standard MH bulb. They are higher in purchase cost, but the efficiency of this light will offset the cost. After three years of running fourteen hours a day, you will save $500 on a CMH over MH.

HPS

If you have flowering plants, you should consider a high-pressure sodium or HPS bulb. This is available in the following power ratings:

-150W

-250W

-400W

-600W

-750W

-1000W

They give an orange/red glow, encouraging the plants to flower.

Examples of flowering plants include:

Tomatoes

Eggplant

Strawberries

Cucumber

Sunflowers

Cannabis

An HPS bulb should give you five years of life, but like every HID light, they will be less effective towards the end of their life.

It is important to get the light setup correct. If you hang it too high, you will lower the PPF. Too low and the light will be too intense, and you will burn the plant.

A 1000W light should have about three feet (0.91 meters) of space between the canopy and the bulb. This also depends on your reflector. If it is narrow, you need to increase the height because the light is more focused.

The footprint of a 1000W light should be 5x5feet (1.5x1.5 meters). This means that you have to place them five feet (1.5 meters) apart from each other if you are using multiple lights.

DE HID

Double-ended high-intensity discharge bulbs are designed with two wires at either side of the glass that accommodates the double- ended tube. These are shorter and thinner than a conventional tube. The result is a higher light density, effectively giving your plants more light and a greater spectrum of light (about twenty-five to thirty percent more efficient than single-ended bulbs).

In short, a double-ended lamp will replicate the sun more effectively. These can be bought at different PAR spectrums.

Double-ended high-intensity discharge

Of course, they are more expensive, and this is a relatively new technology. The bulbs do need to be handled with care, and they can't be hung vertically. If you have the budget and you want to use HID lights, use double-ended ones.

LED

LED lights are becoming one of the most popular choices in many areas of life, and hydroponics is no different.

LED lights use less power than conventional bulbs, generally, last longer and have less heat output.

It's very easy to switch the color spectrum if you want to change to flowering. Some LEDs come with fully adjustable spectrums, while others have a switch between vegetative and flowering.

However, it should be noted that LEDs are generally expensive to purchase, and their better efficiency of supplying the plant with all kinds of light spectrums over HID is often exaggerated.

The primary benefit of LEDs over HID lights is that they produce less heat and could have adjustable PAR spectrums.

The adjusting of the light spectrum is only possible in high-end LEDs, which will make them more expensive.

CFL

CFL or Compact Fluorescent Lamps are surprisingly cost-effective and a popular choice with many indoor growers. They are also an excellent choice for anyone starting in hydroponics as they are one of the cheapest options available.

They are available in different light spectrums but are less powerful than many other light options. It means that they need to be close to the plants.

Hydroponic Grow Systems

There are several different hydroponic systems that you can use, depending on your experience level, available space, investment, and what kind of plants you choose to grow.

Here are the most popular ones, how they work, and how you can establish your system.

Kratky method

The Kratky method is the simplest method of growing your own crop. What makes this system so easy, especially for beginners, is the lack of pumps, electricity, or even wicks.

The main benefit of this system is that once you have set it up, the system runs itself. It is a set and forget system.

You will need:

A mason jar, container, or bucket Seed starter cubes
Growing medium – hydroton works well. Net Pots

That's it, other than water, nutrients, and your testing kit.

Getting Started

First, you should have a seedling ready. The seedling can be cultivated in a seed starter cube. The roots should start to become visible on the bottom of the cube before transplanting.

You can only use one plant per seed starting cube and one per net pot.

You can grow all kinds of plants using the Kratky method, from tomatoes to lettuce. You need a three to five-gallon bucket for tomatoes or cucumbers and a mason jar or a plastic soda bottle for lettuce. I like to use wide mouth mason jars with 3-inch net pots.

The Kratky method is a set and forget growing method you can use on your windowsill. Once the plant starts to grow, the level in the container will drop. As the roots grow, they will keep up with the lowering water level. This will continue until the plant is fully grown. A lettuce needs around sixteen fluid ounces (four hundred and seventy-five milliliters), while the three to five-gallon (eleven to eighteen liter) bucket for tomatoes needs to be refilled often.

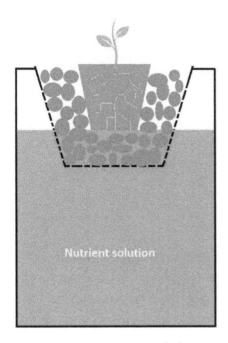

Beginning stage of the Kratky method

The roots will take up the water, and the plant will start to grow. The nutrient solution will drain, but the roots will keep up with the draining water level.

The empty space that is created will provide the roots with oxygen. This will continue until the plant is fully matured, and the water has drained. You need to aim for the plant growth to keep up with the water in the reservoir.

You need to place the setup in a well-lit environment. You must darken the outside of the container with tin foil. This is to discourage algae from growing in the container. Do not use black paper or paint because it will heat the water in the container.

If the water has entirely drained while your plant is not fully grown yet, you need to top-up the water. You need to fill it up halfway, so only half of the roots are submerged.

This system can be established virtually anywhere and needs very little space. I recommend trying this setup for everyone who is starting with hydroponics.

Build the system

Smaller plants:

Take a two or three-inch net pot and put some hydroton at the bottom. Place your seedling with the seed starter cube in the net pot.

Fill the sides with hydroton for the cube to stay upright. Fill the nutrient solution in the container until it touches the bottom of the seed starting cube. Darken the water container so no algae will grow inside.

Bigger plants:

Use a three or five-gallon bucket and use a six-inch net pot with lid.

The process is the same as the smaller plant. The six-inch net pot will be easier for the plant to hold onto because the root system will be much more significant.

If you refill the bucket, only fill it up halfway. This is for the roots to access oxygen. If you were to submerge the whole root system, root rot will occur, and your plant will die.

Wick system

The wick system deserves second place when it comes to easy to make hydroponic systems.

The reason it is so simple is that it doesn't have any moving parts and there is no reliance on electricity.

This is a straightforward system to build and one that will give you a great introduction to hydroponics. It's very similar to the Kratky method but with the addition of a wick.

You'll need

A plastic bottle or tub with lid Two-inch net pots

Seed starter cube

Growing media of your choice Wicking rope

Building the wick system

The premise is simple. Your water container has the water and nutrients your plant needs. Above this sits the plant and a wicking rope that will bring water and nutrients to your plant using the capillary action of the wick.

Start by drilling two-inch holes in the top of your lid. Drill as many as you need to fill the top of the lid. Don't forget that your seedlings will grow, so take that into account. Lettuce should be six to eight inches apart from each other (center to center) depending on the variety.

Start by filling your container with water and your nutrient solution.

Take the two-inch net pots and put the wicking rope trough, so it touches the grow media. Make sure it will touch the roots of the seedling you are going to put in.

Place the lid on the container and place the net cups into the holes you drilled. The wick will be inside the water solution. If done correctly, the wick will deliver the nutrient-rich water to the plant roots. Make this wick touch the bottom of the water reservoir. As the water slowly drains, the wick will provide water to the roots.

It is worth noting that this is a good system for smaller plants, such as lettuce and herbs. However, it is not very practical for more substantial plants like tomatoes, fruiting plants, and peppers. These tend to need a large supply of water and nutrients. The wick system may not be able to deliver them fast enough.

If you choose to create a wick system, you need to consider the right wick material carefully. It is worth testing a few and always soak them first to ensure they provide the most effective wicking action possible.

The best option I have found is using a thick candlewick. They are designed to wick up wax and are made of cotton. They are quite thick too. A roll of six feet will cost you $6. You can reuse these also.

You can make the reservoir as large as you like and increase the number of plants you have accordingly.

It is also important to note that the wick will absorb water and nutrients evenly, but your plant may not. If the air is warmer than usual, the plant will evaporate more water than when it's colder. The evaporation will lead to water being drawn from the wick without the nutrients. This can result in a build-up of nutrients on the wick, which will damage the ability of the wick to work effectively.

Therefore, you should wash or rinse your wick after every harvest to remove excess nutrients (nutrient build-up).

Make sure you block the sun or your grow light from entering the water container. Wrap something around it for the light not to penetrate the container and create algae in the nutrient-rich water. Tinfoil is perfect for this. Avoid using black spray paint is it will heat the water in the container.

Alternative

If you want an even easier method, you can use a plastic bottle and cut off the top. Flip the top of the bottle inside the base and place the wicking rope together with the wicking grow media inside. You can choose to leave the cap on and drill a hole in it or remove the cap entirely. You need to keep an eye on the reservoir as it will drain quickly.

Ebb and flow

This is another system that's easy to set up, but it's worth noting that this is mostly used for starting seeds.

As your experience with hydroponics grows, you'll probably continue to start seeds with this system and then transplant them to a different setup. Commercial farms use this technique for their seedlings.

The ebb and flow system is also referred to as flood and drain, simply because the plant roots are flooded for a few minutes and then drained again.

The point of a flood and drain cycle is exposing the roots to the air while the moisture-holding grow media still provides water and nutrients to the seedlings. It is advised to cut the nutrients in half for seedling because they are sensitive to the nutrients. More on this later in the book.

The flooding and draining happens automatically with a timer.

You'll need

-A container for your plants A water reservoir

-A pump, preferably submersible Timer for the pump

-Tubing for the pump

-A siphon of your choice

-Your choice of growing medium

The plant container is situated above the water reservoir. A pump floods the plant container to a pre-set level, and then it drains back into the reservoir through an overflow pipe.

The pump is turned off by the timer, and the water will flow back to the reservoir through the pressure side of the pump.

Basic sketch of a flood and drain table

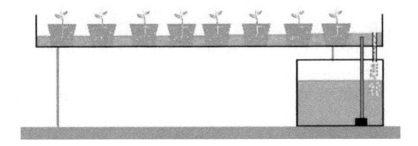

Building the System

Start by drilling two holes in the base of your plant container. One hole is for the water to be delivered to the tray; the other will act as an overflow.

Add your water and nutrients to the water container and turn on your pump. You can time how long it takes to fill the plant container until it overflows. When you shut the pump off, the water will drain back down through the pump pipe and into the water container, creating the ebb and flow.

It should be noted that sunlight or artificial light will probably get to the water in the flood and drain tray, you will need to clean out algae regularly to ensure it isn't using the nutrients and dissolved oxygen meant for the plants.

You can also use another flood and drain system. It uses an overflow and a slow return of the water to the container.

The alternative flood and drain system

This system uses only one hole in the flood tray. The water gets pumped into the tray on a timer like the previous method. When the table is flooding, the water can overflow into the standing pipe back into the reservoir.

The diameter of the overflow pipe should be big enough to return the overflow to your water tank.

When the water reaches the desired level, the timer stops. The pump will shut down, and the water will stop flowing. The water that is still in the flood tray will slowly drain back to the water reservoir through a small hole at the bottom of the overflow pipe. This little hole will return the water slowly to the reservoir.

The hole should be small enough so that the water is allowed to overflow into the standing pipe. The height of the standing pipe will determine the level of the water. The water will slowly drain back into the reservoir.

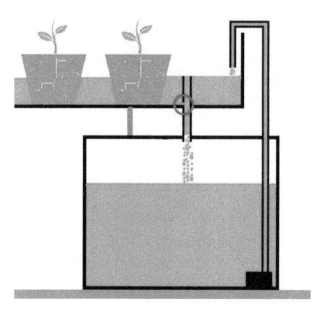

Close up of the slow draining system

DWC system

Most people will try the Kratky and wick system first before using this system.

This is the deep-water culture or DWC system. In some ways, this is very similar to the Kratky system, except that the roots of the plants are submerged into the water all the time.

This system is always designed with an air pump. This makes it more expensive than the Kratky or wick system but very effective at delivering dissolved oxygen to the plant's roots.

Any system that allows the roots to sit directly in the water is referred to as a standard water culture. For it to classify as a deep-water culture system, the water should be at least twelve inches (thirty centimeters) deep. The depth of the water will serve as a temperature buffer.

There are two main DWC systems:

Bucket DWC (hobbyist)

Floating rafts (commercial systems)

We are going to start explaining the five-gallon bucket DWC.

You'll need

-A five-gallon bucket or larger container

-Lid with six-inch net pot

-Seed starter cube Air Pump

Flexible hose for the air pump

-One airstone

-Your growing media (hydroton is preferred)

Building the system

Before you start creating your DWC hydroponic system, you should think about what you intend to grow. Medium-sized plants like tomatoes or peppers do best in a bucket DWC system.

You need to cut or drill a small hole near the top of the bucket. It should be big enough to take your flexible air hose. The hole is drilled at the top of the bucket and not in the lid. This will make it easier for you to remove the lid from time to time to check the water level and roots.

Now put one air stone at the bottom of your water reservoir.

You can now connect your airline to your air stone and the other end to your pump.

Use a six-inch net pot lid that will fit a standard five-gallon bucket. Put the washed grow media (hydroton) in the net pot and put your seedling in the middle.

Now you can fill your bucket with nutrient-rich water. You are aiming to get the base of the roots submerged, just like the Kratky method.

Once you've got this right, you can draw a line just above the water line inside your container. It is advisable to draw several lines around the container. This will ensure that the lines don't just rub off. These lines will be used as reference to fill the container back up when the water is being drained.

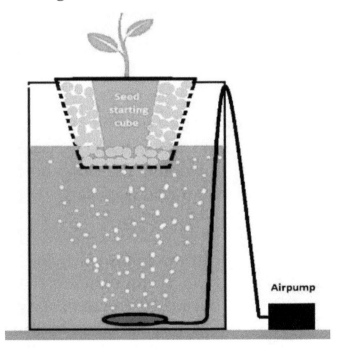

Deepwater culture in a bucket

Do a final check of the nutrients and pH level and then put the lid on with your plant in the net pot.

If your bucket is placed outside in the sun, you should wrap it with tin foil to discourage algae from growing inside. Do not spray paint it black because the water in the bucket will heat up quickly.

Algae need three things to flourish: light, nutrients, and water. You need to block out the light to your water to remove one of these things from the equation and reduce the likelihood of algae.

Tip: If you are struggling to take your lid on and off to check the pH, etc. Cut a small hole in it and use a pipette to extract a little water for testing. The small hole will make it easier to top up the water if necessary.

In the following image, you can see four buckets that are using this system. I would correct the setup by drilling a small hole in the bucket itself instead of passing the air tube through the net pot.

I previously mentioned that there is another method for deep water culture that is mainly used in commercial systems. It is called floating rafts.

Floating raft hydroponics uses Styrofoam rafts that float on a body of water. Just like the bucket system, the roots are submerged in the water, and air stones are placed underneath.

The Styrofoam material needs to be food grade. Most Styrofoam insulation panels have a fire-retardant coating that will leach into the water and contaminate it.

If you build this system, don't expose the water to concrete because it will alter the pH level in the system. Instead, choose twenty mils (0.5mm) pond liner.

Floating rafts can only be used with small crops like lettuce. The bigger the plant, the harder it is for the rafts to float and the more space it needs.

You can also use the floating raft technique in your home system. You can do this by cutting an IBC tote or by using a tub.

The advantage of deep-water culture is that the temperature remains stable because of the large volume of water. When the water drains, the floating rafts will lower with the water level.

Drip system

You may have already come across a drip system with conventional soil-potted plants. This is a very popular option because it is very easy to add or remove plants and automate the system.

The principle behind this type of hydroponics system is to get the nutrient-rich water to the roots, by dripping it slowly onto the plant roots.

There are two methods of drip systems:

-Recirculating

-Non-recirculating

Most drip systems are designed as recirculating. A recirculating system pumps the water from the reservoir to the plants and has a drainage system that allows the water to drain back into the reservoir, effectively allowing the water to go in a circle.

This is an efficient approach as water loss is minimized, only that which transpires from the plants or evaporates into the atmosphere is lost. You'll need a minimal amount of water to top up the system.

In contrast, the non-recirculating system doesn't allow the water to return to the reservoir. This is why they are also known as "run to waste" systems.

This may seem like a wasteful option as the water will need to be replenished regularly. However, this is a very popular option for commercial farmers because the costs involved are low.

The non-recirculating system is run with a top-up reservoir. The delivery of nutrient-rich water is carefully measured, so no water and nutrients are lost. This minimizes waste.

You will have to mix another batch with a predetermined ratio of nutrients and water. This makes the non-recirculating system easy to operate.

Drip systems will be used in various systems like:

-Drip irrigation tray NFT

-Dutch buckets

-Vertical towers and A-frames

I will first explain how you can create a drip irrigation system in a tray.

You'll need

-Big tray for the plants

-Water reservoir Submersible

-pump Timer

-Drip irrigation materials (listed separately)

-Growing media

Building the system

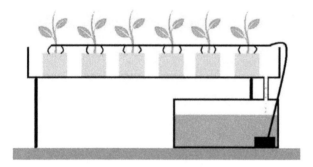

A drip table system

The system uses a pump to build pressure in an irrigation tube.

The irrigation tube is a standard garden irrigation line that can be bought from your local hardware store like home depot or lowes. This is what you will need for the drip system:

Mainline: ¾ inch (1.9 cm) tubing

Secondary line: ¼ inch (0.6 cm) tubing

Hole puncher Drip emitter

Emitter stake (2 per plant)

Endcap for ¾ inch (1.9 cm) tube

If you do not want to use an endcap or zip ties, you can use a T splitter and create a loop without end.

Top view of a ring loop drip system

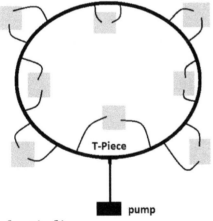

When setting up the system, you should use a large tray to put your pots in. You can use a professional flood tray like the following image. A cheaper alternative is making your own using plastic liner.

Professional flood tray

This tray is used to collect runoff from the drip emitters. It will collect the water and return it to the nutrient reservoir.

The following image shows the setup with a non-recirculating or drain to waste system.

Drain to waste system with tray

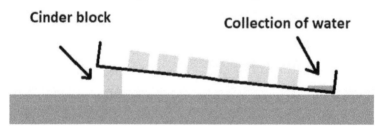

Don't forget: The better the water retention of the growing media, the more tolerant the plants will be of delayed watering or other issues. I recommend using Rockwool.

How to install drip emitters

Above the plants, you'll need to run the drip line and puncture two holes right next to each plant. Insert the drip emitter and connect it to the irrigation line. Then add the drip stake.

Connection of drip emitters

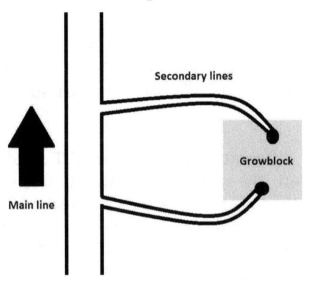

Excess water will make its way down through the growing media and end up in the tray. From there, the water returns or gets removed from the tray.

Your pump will be connected to a timer, which should run three to five times a day for five minutes.

The next step is to fill your reservoir with water and test the system. Once you're happy, add the plants and the nutrients.

NFT

NFT stands for Nutrient Film Technique. It's another simple design but is especially useful if you're growing lettuce or other quick- growing plants.

However, you should be aware that this type of system uses shallow tubes or gutters. Plants with extensive roots can block the flow of water, causing you issues.

There are many different designs for the NFT system, but the basics are the same. Nutrient-rich water is pumped around the system, along the gutters where the roots of the plants can touch the water and extract the nutrients they need. The water flow will need to be constant, and the channel needs to be shallow.

Lettuce in an NFT system Image from

You'll need

-Nutrient solution reservoir

-Submersible pump

-NFT channels Return pipes

-Drip irrigation parts

How to Build It

Start by deciding where you want your reservoir. This is the hardest part of the system to move. You can then take your first piece of guttering and drill two-inch holes along one side of it each eight inches for lettuce (center to center). If you are using shallow gutter pipes, you can drop the seed starter cubes right in the gully without net pots. If you use a round pipe, you need net pots to hold the seedling in place.

Put the gutters up on a rack with a four-degree decline. You can put several channels next to each other.

Next, add a return line back to the water reservoir. The return line can be placed under the gutters for convenience.

Although this system is very effective at getting nutrient-rich water to your plants, the plants will quickly start to suffer if the water flow is disrupted for any reason.

The film needs to be very thin. Don't create a DFT system (deep flow technique). The advantage of an NFT system is that the water doesn't need additional aeration because roots can access the oxygen.

In the U.S., you can purchase a rain gutter downspout, which is flat on the bottom. A three-inch by two inches downspout is perfect for a cost-efficient NFT channel. Holes should be spaced eight inches (twenty centimeters) apart from each other for growing lettuce heads. Start with four inches (ten centimeters) from the side and then eight inches in between the following holes. Allow eight inches between each NFT gutter.

The main PVC line after your pump should be 1 ½ inch (three centimeters) in diameter. From there, you go to a ¾ inch (one point nine centimeters) PVC pipe. From this one point, three-quarter-inch (nine centimeters) line, you drill the holes to accommodate the feeding drip lines. Use a maximum of 10 drip lines on each ¾ inch PVC pipe.

Dripline setup for NFT

Drill 3/8 inch holes with a drill bit and use 3/8 inch grommets to keep the feeder lines in place. The outer edge of the feeder line will press against the grommet, which will make a waterproof seal. The feeder line will be drip irrigation tubing of 3/8 inch and will have a flow of

0.13 gallons (0.5 liters) per minute per tube.

People on the internet suggest that the best flow rate for NFT hydroponics is one to two liters per minute. However, studies show that flow rates of 20 liters per hour or 0.33 liters per minute have the best crop yield.

3/8 inch (0.9 cm) grommets are sold online

The type of gutter

In commercial systems, you will only see flat channels. This is to increase the contact area for the roots to absorb water. Most home growers use a three-inch drainpipe.

You can reduce the flowrate if you're dealing with seedlings and then gradually increase it as the plants grow.

Dutch bucket

The dutch bucket is another drip system that is perfect for growing plants that have more prominent root structures like tomatoes, cucumbers, or bell peppers. It is easy to establish, and more buckets can be added when you need it in the future.

Before we get stuck into making a dutch bucket system, it is a good idea to gain an understanding of the difference between drip systems and the dutch bucket system.

The two systems are mostly the same: both feed the plant's water and nutrients via a drip system. The main difference is that a dutch bucket system uses buckets, usually three to five-gallon buckets, hence the name. The most common grow media options are perlite, hydroton, and river rock.

Growers prefer a recirculating dutch bucket setup. This means the excess water returns to the main water reservoir.

Another setup is non-recirculating. This is when the flow of the water is properly dosed, so there is no need for a return line to the water container. Non-recirculating systems are cheaper to build but need other nutrient dosing than recirculating. The proper dosing of nutrients for non-recirculating systems can be found on the website of the manufacturer for the particular nutrients you are using.

Let's create a re-circulating dutch bucket drip system. You will be able to find all the parts you need at your local hardware store.

You'll need

-Three, four, or five-gallon buckets

-One inch uniseal fittings or grommets for your buckets
-Growing Media – Perlite, river rock or a mix of both

-A water reservoir of at least fifteen gallons (depending on the system)

-A submersible pump

-Poly tubing ½ inch mainline and ¼ inch feeding line -
-Some bricks and wooden planks

-8-gallon drip emitters (2 per bucket) One inch elbows for the drain

-1 inch PVC pipe for the drain

-Two-inch PVC pipe for the main drain

Getting Started

First, you need to estimate how high the dutch buckets will be. You need to elevate the bucket line for the nutrients to return to your water reservoir by gravity.

Then, place some bricks on top of each other and create an area where you can put your buckets on using planks to connect the gap between the bricks.

You will have to drill a hole three inches (seven centimeters) from the bottom of the bucket. Use a one-inch hole saw and clear the edges with sanding paper. Take the one-inch uniseal and put it in the hole. Push your one inch PVC piping trough this uniseal and connect the PVC pipe to a ninety-degree elbow. Do this for all the buckets you have.

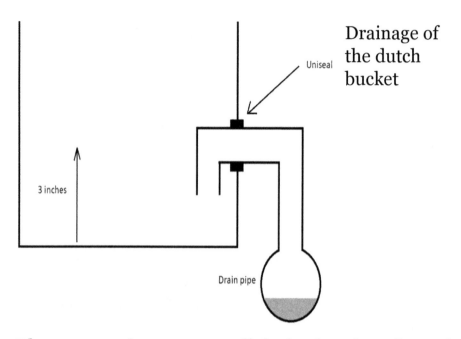

The next step is to connect all the buckets into the main drain line. This will be two-inch PVC piping. Now you have made the return to your water reservoir.

Next, we need to create the water flow to the buckets. We do this by using a half-inch irrigation line that is made from poly tubing. Run it to your buckets and punch a hole in it with the hole puncher just like you would with a regular drip system.

Put a quarter-inch irrigation line in this hole and run it to your dutch buckets. Then add 2-gallon drip emitters and place them close to the root of the plant. If your buckets are white, add tin foil to block any sunlight.

Do a leak test before adding the media. If there are no leaks, you can add the washed media to the buckets.

Most people use lids to avoid algae on top of the bucket. Alternatively, you can bury the drip emitters in the perlite for about one inch. This means there is about one inch of dry perlite on top, which will inhibit algae creation.

River rock or hydroton is used to let the dutch bucket drain better.

That's it. You are ready to test your system. Turn on your pump and make sure every drip emitter is working.

It is important to note that the pump does not need to run continually: fifteen minutes three to four times a day should suffice, although you may wish to tweak this depending on your local temperature. If the media gets dry quickly, increase the time.

Easy cleanout tips:

When you have harvested the fruit from the plant, stop the water flow to the dutch buckets. Let it sit for a few days for the plant to absorb all the moisture that is inside the bucket. This makes it easier to clean them out later.

Keep the perlite in a strainer bag to keep it separated from the river rock or hydroton. This makes it easier to clean and separate after the harvest.

Vertical system

The vertical hydroponics system is a great space saver and can be made in many different forms. The vertical A system uses NFT channels for the plants while the vertical towers use custom grow towers or three-inch PVC pipes. Both use drip irrigation.

Vertical A-frame

Of course, you don't need to go small. The following design has a footprint of six feet by ten feet. You could grow as many as one hundred and sixty-eight plants in this space!

```
12 gutters x 14 plants per gutter = 168
```

You'll need

-Wood to make the A-frame

-Twelve times three-inch gutter pipe each nine feet long
-Three-inch gutter pipe brackets

-Three quarter inch uniseals or grommets

-Quarter-inch poly tubing

-Pump

-Three quarter inch pipe for the drain lines

-A container as a water reservoir

Getting Started

Start by creating your A-frame. You will need a piece of wood at four feet, then two pieces of wood attached to this and joined together at the top. This creates the A-frame at each end. A middle support is also a good idea. You will then need to join the two ends together with several battens of wood, three or four on each side.

The vertical A-Frame

You can also add cross braces to help ensure this is a sturdy, free- standing A-frame.

You are now ready to install gutter clamps along each of the downward posts. You will want three braces on each post to support six gutter pipes.

It is crucial to make sure these are at a four-degree decline. Do not let more water sit in the channels. Otherwise, you will be using the DFT system (deep flow technique). A DFT system is a DWC system in an NFT system.

You can now cut two-inch holes in your PVC pipes to accommodate the net pots: you should have twelve PVC pipes measuring nine feet each; that is six on each side if your plant spacing is eight inches

Place the PVC pipes into the clamps and add the net pots to each of the holes. You can use Rockwool or alternative growing media in the net pots ready for planting.

You will now need to add drains to the end of the PVC piping. Drill a hole with a 1.25 hole saw so you can fit a three quarter inch uniseal at the bottom. Run three quarter inch pipe straight down into a collection gutter. Attach pipes to the guttering by sliding them through the hole and making sure they stick up inside the pipe as far as one to one and a half inch. This will allow the water to drain back to the reservoir.

You will also need to place an end cap on your guttering to prevent the water from coming out. Make it so you can unplug the endcap so it is easy to clean out if need be.

Your submersible pump needs to go into the reservoir. From here, you will have to connect piping to the middle of your A-Frame. From here, you use the same grommets that are used in NFT systems.

Next, you need to add a small valve to the irrigation line to control the flow of the water. This is to regulate the flow because the bottom line will put out more water than the top line because of gravity and resistance. Tune the flow of the twelve flexible lines for the flow to be equal in each gutter.

You should test this part of the system before adding the seeds, seedlings, or plants. Select a pump using the guide in this book.

The pump needs to run continuously. It is important to note that the more levels you have in a vertical system, the higher the head height, the higher the power of the pump that is required.

Vertical towers

Another option worth considering is hydroponic towers. You'll need to decide how many towers you want; this will be directly related to your budget and the space you have available.

A seven-foot tube has slots for approximately twenty plants. Therefore, if you start with six tubes, you will have enough space to grow one hundred and twenty plants.

The great thing about this tube is they need a minimal footprint. You will need to construct a frame that supports the tubes. You can make these tubes yourself by making a slit in the PVC piping and heating it with a hot air gun and inserting a mold (two-inch pipe) the size of a net pot while the plastic is still hot.

A Vertical tower

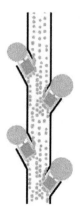

The water will be supplied to the top of the grow towers and will drip into a collection gutter back to your reservoir (comparable with dutch buckets).

The towers need to be hung from a frame. You can make this frame with wood and metal wire. You can attach these towers to the frame.

Similar to the A-Frame NFT system, you will need to use three quarter inch irrigation line as the mainline and attach a smaller quarter inch feeder line into the towers.

You can increase water distribution by using a wick inside the vertical tower.

Aeroponics

Aeroponics is a great way to use hydroponics in a futuristic way. I only recommend aeroponics if you already have some experience with hydroponics. Aeroponics is not easy, and there are a lot of things that can go wrong, like clogging up of the nozzles. Aeroponics systems are popular with cloning.

There are two types of aeroponics systems. The first one we are going to discuss is the low-pressure system. After this, we will talk about the high-pressure system.

Low-pressure system

A low-pressure system isn't true aeroponics. With low-pressure aeroponics, you don't create the fine mist that high-pressure aeroponics does. However, hobbyists are coming up with an alternative for the expensive high-pressure systems.

This system that is used by many hobby growers is a fifty-five-gallon plastic drum. Holes are made in the drum to accommodate forty-five- degree elbows. These elbows will fit the net pots for your plants.

The roots will start to grow on the inside of the barrel, where they get periodically sprayed by gardening nozzles that are pressurized by a pump.

The water drains from the barrel to a reservoir where it is easy to mix the nutrients and measure nutrient levels.

Low-pressure barrel aeroponics

You need to select a pump that can provide pressure for the system. Take the flow rate of a nozzle and multiply it by the amount you have in your system. Take the head height of the system into consideration too. You need to oversize your pump by at least a factor of two to get the desired pressure.

Example:

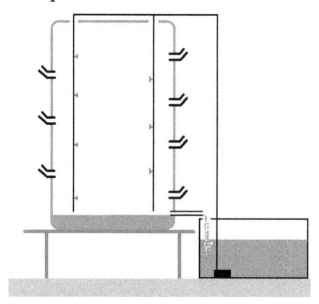

You got ten nozzles with a flow rate of thirty gallons per hour at 20psi each. You would need a pump that can provide three hundred gallons per hour without head height taken into consideration. Multiply this by two because we need to have pressure inside of the piping. 300 gallons per hour x 2 = 600 gallons per hour.

Next, we consider head height. For this example, it is going to be four feet. We then draw the horizontal line first and then the vertical line on six hundred gallons per hour. We see that we need to use the one thousand gallons per hour pump.

The nozzles are regular gardening nozzles. Make sure you use nozzles that spray one hundred and eighty degrees. There are forty- five and ninety degrees, but they do not mist the entire barrel. You need to use gardening sprinklers (plastic) instead of the brass nozzles. The brass nozzles are only for high-pressure systems.

High-pressure system

High-pressure aeroponics is an effective technique to ensure the roots get all the oxygen they need for healthy growth.

A high-pressure system costs more money than a low-pressure system and is mainly used in commercial indoor farms or cloning machines.

There are four key components to any high-pressure aeroponics system:

1. The Pump

In many ways, this is the heart of your system; without it, you won't get the misting effect you need. The pump raises the pressure in your system, allowing the misting nozzles to work correctly.

An excellent guide to pump pressure is to ensure that your pump can deliver a minimum of 60-80psi (4 to 5.5 bars), the misting nozzles won't work with pressure lower than this. The pumps used are diaphragm pumps.

Your pump must be intended to deliver high pressure. Not any pump will do. Most pumps have a built-in pressure switch. The pressure switch will shut the pump off at the highest pressure the pump is rated for. If there is no pressure switch, the membrane of the pump will break, making your pump useless.

The pumps used in high-pressure aeroponics are self-priming pumps.

2.   Pressure Tank

You've probably seen a pressure tank on your home water system. They help to maintain the pressure of your water.

There are two segments inside the tank: the bladder and pressurized air. Water fills the tank, which compacts the air, increasing the pressure on the bladder. This maintains pressure for the system. The flow rate of the water into the tank will control the pressure rate.

It will act as a pressure buffer, so your pump doesn't need to turn on and off every few seconds. You don't need one, but it is much better for the lifespan of your pump.

3. Misting Nozzles

The misting nozzles have tiny holes, called an orifice. They are as little as 12,000 of an inch! For this system, the best idea is to have holes of 10,000 of an inch.

The idea is that the pressure of the water going through the misting nozzle converts the water into a mist. This mist is then sprayed into the root area of your plant, giving them water, nutrients, and oxygen. In short, everything they need.

4. Filter

Because the orifice of the misting nozzle is tiny, filters are used to prevent clogging. A filter of thirty microns will be enough to avoid clogging up of the nozzles.

It is worth noting that the plants sit on a box with their roots inside the box. The misters are in the box, and there will need to be a drain point, allowing water to return to the water reservoir where the pump sits.

Fogponics

Fogponics works in a similar way to aeroponics, but this type of system uses fog instead of misting. It is mainly used to create clones. The fog is created by an ultrasonic device that floats on the water. The vibration evaporates the water.

This leads us to its main drawbacks which are:

-The water in the container will warm up.

-The container needs to be enclosed for the fog to stay trapped inside the container.

To create a fogponics system, you will need:

-A storage container

-An ultrasonic vibration device

-Net pots or cloning collars

A small storage container that can hold ten gallons is ideal for this setup. You will need one with a lid that you can close.

You will need to drill a few 2⅛ inch holes in the lid to put in your net pots. If you are using this system for clones, these holes can be close together. If you are using it for lettuce, you need to use the appropriate plant spacing (approx. eight inches/ twenty centimeters).

If you are using clones with net pots, you should cut the bottom of the net pot out. This is to accommodate the stem of the clone to go down. If you have special cloning pots, you don't need to do this, as there will be an opening at the bottom.

You then have to use a foam or collar insert, it will stay in place and the net cup will not fall into your tank. The stalk of the clone slides through the foam, protruding into the tote (but not submerged). Ideally, you need two nodes available under the cloning collar. A node is a place where the leaves are appearing on the stem.

You will need to cut an extra hole for the wiring of your ultrasonic fogger. You can cover up the hole by using cloning foam around the cable, so the fog doesn't escape.

Next, you will need to add the fogger. Look for a fogger that puts at least 400mL/H of water into the air. It will consume around fifteen to twenty watts. Once the fogger is connected, you can use a one hour on, one hour off cycle. There is no pump needed in this system.

You'll need to check the water level, the nutrients, and temperature regularly.

Starting seeds

It is most satisfying when you plant a seed and nurture it until it becomes a full-grown plant and provides you with the intended harvest.

Of course, it takes more effort to grow a plant from seed than it does from a seedling, you need to decide if this is your preferred method and discover the best way of starting seeds.

Hydroponics is an excellent system for starting seeds as you have complete control over the elements your seeds are exposed to.

Seeds vs. Seedlings

For your first attempt at hydroponics, it is quicker to plant seedlings. However, controlling all the elements of the growing process includes controlling the seeds. If you decide to plant seeds, you will have complete control over the type and quality of the seed you plant.

Put simply, you can have any variety of seed but not necessarily any variety of seedling. Seeds are generally easier to get hold of then seedlings.

The other consideration is the growing media. In hydroponics, you avoid using soil. However, unless you have a hydroponic center near you, the seedlings you purchase are likely to be grown in soil. This means carefully removing the soil to avoid contamination of your system. Unfortunately, washing them can damage the roots of the seedling.

Besides, seeds are cheaper than seedlings, allowing you more opportunities for failure without breaking the bank.

With proper planning and equipment, you are better off growing the plants from seed.

Starting Your Seeds

The best way to start seeds is to use a seed starter cube. A cube the size of one and a half inch will fit perfectly in a two-inch net pot. These small cubes are capable of holding water while air can reach the roots, which is the most important while germinating seeds.

First, you need to soak your grow cubes in chlorine or chloramine free water with a pH of 5.5. Water from your tap will be around 7-8 pH. You most likely need to use a pH down solution.

Getting the chlorine out of your tap water is quite easy. Let it sit for one day for the chlorine to evaporate. If you want it to evaporate faster, you can use an air stone to air the chlorine out much quicker.

If your water company uses chloramine, you need a reverse osmosis filter to remove the chloramine. Note that not every reverse osmosis filter can remove chloramine. Chloramine can't be aired out and needs to be filtered. If you do not have a reverse osmosis filter available, you can use one thousand mg (one gram) of vitamin C (ascorbic acid) per forty gallons (one hundred and fifty liters) of water.

Use a tray to soak the cubes, pour the water on top, and let it sit for a few minutes. Once most of the water is absorbed, you need to drain the rest of the water. Do not squeeze the cubes. This will remove air pockets inside the cubes.

The next step is dropping your seeds into the holes. This can be a big task if you need to do a lot of seeds. Commercial growers use pelleted seeds and a vacuum seeder to speed this process up. Pelleted seed is a seed that is wrapped in clay. it is bigger, thus easier to handle.

You could also use a toothpick and dip the tip in some water. This will make the seed stick to the toothpick, as shown in the following image.

Placing the seed into the seed starter cube

If the holes of the grow media are preventing you from dropping the seed in, use a pen or a toothpick to open the hole back up.

You can use more than one seed per hole if the germination rate is bad. I always use two seeds per hole. When both seeds germinate, I keep the best one and use scissors to remove the bad one.

Next, place your humidity dome on top of the tray to keep the seed starter cubes moist. Generally, the seeds don't need water until they have germinated.

If you notice that your seed starter cubes are drying out, you can pour some more water in the tray. Don't forget to drain the rest of the water.

Once the seeds start showing its first two leaves, you need to put it under a light source. This will provide the plant with the energy they need to grow. If you experience that the stems are growing long (stretching). It means that your plant is reaching for light. Increase the light on the seedlings to avoid this stretching. Do not use red light on seedlings. White fluorescents that are 6500K are perfect.

After ten days, you can transplant them to your system. If you are growing in a greenhouse, it can take fifteen days in winter.

Heat mats will increase germination during colder weather. The mats are placed under the seedling tray to warm up the seed starting cubes. Setting the heat mat to 68°F is recommended.

Recap:

1. Soak your seed starting cubes in chlorine or chloramine free water. Distilled water is even better. Make sure the pH is around 5.5.

2. Put the seed starting cubes in a tray.

3. Put the seed in the holes of the seed starter cubes.

4. Cover the seed starting cubes with a humidity dome.

5. Set the heat mat to 68°F (20°C) and place it under the tray.

6. Once sprouts appear, water them from the bottom with one quarter nutrient strength. The cubes will wick up the water.

7. Place them under T5 fluorescent lights. The humidity dome is still on the tray.

8. When you see four leaves and the roots are developing out of the seed starting cubes, it is time to transplant them to your growing system.

Nutrients during seeding

Seeds don't need nutrients initially as they are self-contained. However, you can give them a quarter-strength solution, compared to what you are using in your adult plant hydroponic system. More on nutrients later in the book.

Cloning

When you hear the word 'cloning', you probably think of science fiction and all sorts of adverse outcomes when humans mess with the natural order of things.

However, plant clones are used a lot around the world. In essence, a plant clone is simply a cutting from a plant that is allowed to grow by itself. The new plant has the same characteristics as the original plant. Cloning can be used to ensure all your plants have a good yield. Take your clone from an existing plant that yields highly.

But, it is more than just an efficient way to get healthy, high-yield plants. Cloning is considerably faster than purchasing seeds.

Of course, successful cloning takes a little more knowledge than just planting. You will need to make sure the conditions are just right. A small aeroponics or fogponics system like we discussed earlier in the book is perfect for growing out clones.

The roots temperature should be around 68°F (20°C). Air temperature should be 64-77°F (18-25°C).

Light must be diluted and never direct.

You only need a partial nutrient solution. Use twenty-five percent of the standard recommended nutrients for the plant.

You can use rooting liquids like clonex from hydrodynamics to help the roots to become established.

The Cloning Procedure

To prepare your cutting, you will need to find a healthy plant and then remove the best-looking growing tip. There should be no more than two sets of leaves. If you plan on cloning tomatoes, use the suckers.

When removing the soon to be clone, you should cut at a forty-five- degree angle to increase its area of nutrient uptake. The clone needs this because it doesn't have roots yet. Allow two nodes on each clone. A node is a place where a leaf appears. You must remove the bottom leaves of the clone to increase its likeliness of developing roots.

Now place it into a cloning sponge. It will take between seven to fifteen days for the roots to develop.

When roots have developed, you can transplant them to your hydroponics system of choice.

The reason for leaving only two leaves on the clone is because the plant still evaporates water to continue photosynthesis. Because there is no root, the plant uptake of water will be limited.

Reducing light during this stage will reduce the need for water. Only increase light exposure when roots are developing.

Best plants for Hydroponics

It should be possible to grow almost anything hydroponically. After all, you are supplying all the nutrients the plant needs.

Here are the growth factors for plants:

-Temperature

-Humidity

-Nutrients

-Water Oxygen

-Co2 Wind

-Radiation (light)

Failing to supply one or more in this list will result in slower growth or a failed crop. Make sure you always have these eight elements optimized to have the quickest growing crop.

However, as with anything, some plants are better suited to this type of system, while others are not. Here are some that do exceptionally well in a hydroponic system:

Lettuce

This is potentially the easiest plant to grow and a great one for anyone new to hydroponics. They can adapt to any hydroponics system, need just ten to fourteen hours of light a day. They are surprisingly flexible regarding temperature. It prefers temperatures between 45°F and 70°F (7-21°C).

It is a fast-growing plant that will help you feel successful on your first try. You should plant them between six to eight inches (fifteen to twenty centimeters) apart. Lettuce does very well in Kratky, NFT, and deep-water culture.

Lettuce in an NFT system

Tomatoes

Tomatoes are an excellent choice for the Dutch bucket system. It should be noted that tomatoes prefer warmer weather. You may also need artificial lighting to ensure they have enough light. Besides, you'll need to use trellises because tomato plants will grow tall.

Removing suckers

To boost your yield and improve the quality of your tomato plant, it is a good idea to learn how to remove the suckers properly.

Each of the suckers will drain the energy from the main plant instead of allowing the nutrition to be absorbed. If you don't remove them, then you will have more foliage, which will lead to blockage of light to the flowering plant — actually reducing your yield compared to pruned suckers.

It is a good idea to do this when the sucker is small, it will minimize the risk of infection. Look for a place where more than one stem leaves the main stem. You will need to remove the middle stem, leaving just one.

It is also a good idea to remove any leaves that appear in the first two feet of the plant once it is matured. This will reduce the amount of diseases.

Spinach

Growing it hydroponically means you can grow it throughout the year. It is quite easy to grow, and very tolerant of temperature changes.

You should aim for the same spacing as lettuce, although you can plant a little denser if needed. It is comfortable in a temperature range of 50-80°F (10-27°C), making it easy to look after. Spinach takes about one and a half to two months to grow from seed to harvest. Spinach can be cut to regrow again up to three times.

Strawberry

Strawberries do exceptionally well in a hydroponics system. Unlike many fruit plants, they flourish throughout the year with minimum input.

Don't forget that if you start with seeds, it can take a long time before you to get any fruit.

It is normal to start from runners, which can be purchased throughout the year. They will need between eight to twelve hours of light per day and need temperatures between 60-80°F (15-27°C) with a slightly lower night temperature.

Bell peppers

Bell peppers need to be spaced eighteen to twenty-four inches apart to ensure the whole plant gets the nutrition and light it needs. The plant does need warmer temperatures like tomatoes, and you will need to provide trellises as the plants can get very heavy.

It is also a good idea to make sure they have between fourteen to eighteen hours of light every day.

These grow best in a dutch bucket system.

Arugula

You may know this as 'rocket salad' and be accustomed to including it in your salad.

You will find these are a good option for Kratky, NFT, or DWC systems.

Kale

This leafy vegetable is surprisingly easy to grow in your hydroponics system.

Kale does very well in a DWC system, Kratky, and NFT.

Herbs

Almost any herb will do well in a hydroponic system. For example, chives, mint, lavender, parsley, rosemary, basil, and coriander.

Herbs do very well in an NFT system. They respond well to the constant flow of water. Keep an eye on the roots, so they don't get too big and block the channel.

Flowers

Virtually any flower can be grown hydroponically. Although they may not give you edible produce, they can be sold. Especially as you can grow them all year round in a greenhouse.

Flowers of all shapes and sizes tend to do very well in a dutch bucket system and NFT depending on their size.

Plants to avoid

Here are the ones you should avoid trying to grow hydroponically:

Pumpkins

Pumpkins love sunshine and well-drained, pH-neutral soil.

Perhaps most importantly is the fact that they have large root clusters and spread quickly. Thus, making them difficult to grow in most hydroponic systems.

Squash

Squash grows at the base of the plant, which means it may be resting on damp growing media. This is likely to encourage fungal growth.

Besides, squash is generally a large plant with a minimal yield. There are much better ways to utilize the space in your hydroponics system.

Zucchini

This is a large plant, which means it will need plenty of support. It needs more nutrients than other plants, and will not give as great of a yield for the space.

You would need to maintain the temperature around 75°F (24°C), even throughout the night. It will also dry out very quickly if it doesn't get enough water and nutrients.

Potatoes

Most root vegetables are not well suited for hydroponic systems. Potatoes are such a case.

The cost of the crop will be low compared to your effort in growing it.

Radish

Some plants will grow well, but they are still not a good option, radish is one of these. You would need to choose the right media to grow these hydroponically, and you will find the cost is probably higher than purchasing it at the store.

Shrubs

This isn't what most people think of when starting a hydroponics system, but it is worth noting that shrubs, corn, and similar plants have a large root system. You would need a massive water reservoir and planting container to accommodate these needs which wouldn't be a viable option.

Nutrient solutions

There has been extensive discussion about nutrients and how important they are for your plants. Now is the time to take a look at what nutrients a plant needs.

Macronutrients and Micronutrients

Your plants need nutrition to grow successfully. However, you may not realize that there are two types of nutrients: macro and micro.

Macronutrients are, unsurprisingly, in much higher demand. This is because they are essential for the correct function of the cells within the plant.

Micronutrients are compounds that are needed in minimal quantities, especially when compared to macronutrients.

Let's take a look at what these are in more detail. This will help you to establish what nutrients should be introduced to your hydroponics system.

Primary Macronutrients (NPK)

There are three primary macronutrients which are essential for the growth of any plant. These are:

-Nitrogen (N)

-Phosphorus (P)

-Potassium (K)

Nitrogen (N)

It doesn't matter if you are growing hydroponically or in soil, your plants will need nitrogen. This compound is available in two forms, NO_3 and NH_4.

NH_3 is nitrate and is absorbed by plants slowly. It is an essential part of the synthesis of amino acids, which helps the plant to mature and grow.

In contrast, NH_4 is effectively ammonia and will damage the pathways inside your plants, potentially causing your plant to die.

Nitrogen is added to the nutrient mix in the form of calcium nitrate (more on this later).

Phosphorus (P)

Phosphorus is a compound that all living creatures need. It is part of your DNA and provides energy transfer between cells, making it an essential part of photosynthesis. You will find phosphorus in plant fertilizers, either as phosphoric acid or phosphates. It is particularly important during the flowering stage of plant growth. Without enough phosphorus, your plants will become stunted and blotchy.

Potassium (K)

Potassium is a primary macronutrient as it helps the plant to utilize other nutrients. It also helps seeds mature, flowers to grow, and increase fruit yields.

Secondary Macronutrients

Secondary macronutrients are needed in the nutrient mix but not at the quantity that the primary macronutrients are required.

Secondary macronutrients include: Calcium (Ca)

Magnesium (Mg) Sulfur (S)

Micronutrients

Micronutrients are only needed in small quantities. But they are essential for plant growth. These include:

Chlorine (Cl) Copper (Cu) Manganese (Mn) Boron (B)

Iron (Fe) Molybdenum (Mo) Zinc (Zn)

Liquid Nutrients

Let's start with a liquid solution that most beginners use. These are the general hydroponics flora series.

All nutrient mixes come with instructions. These will be different varying on the brand. The mixing ratios can be found online or simply on the bottle they come in like this one. If we look at the label of the Flora series, we see the following information:

Label of the flora series

Basic Applications Table	FloraGro		FloraMicro		FloraBloom	
	tsp/gallon	ml/100 liters	tsp/gallon	ml/100 liters	tsp/gallon	ml/100 liters
Cuttings and Seedlings	1/4	33	1/4	33	1/4	33
General Purpose – Mild Vegetative	1	132	1	132	1	132
Aggressive Vegetative Growth	3	396	2	264	1	132
Transition to Bloom	2	264	2	264	2	264
Blooming and Ripening	1	132	2	264	3	396

We must look at the basic applications table. If you are growing leafy greens, you need to use the 'general purpose – mild vegetative' nutrient mix.

If you are growing tomatoes, you first must use the 'general purpose

– mild vegetative' mix. This is to encourage foliage growth. When the plant produces flowers, you need to switch to the 'blooming and ripening' nutrient blend.

How to mix liquid nutrients

Take water from your tap, rainwater, or distilled water and use a TDS meter to give you the amount of total dissolved solids in your water. You need to remember this number for later use.

Tap water should be around 100-400ppm while distilled water is less than 25ppm.

You need to know how much water you are going to use. Knowing the amount of water you have will be crucial to the dosing of the nutrients. This is how I mix my nutrients with the flora series:

1. I fill a 5-gallon bucket with tap water and let it sit overnight to air out the chlorine.

2. I read the PPM of my tap water with a TDS meter and see it has 350PPM.

3. I am growing lettuce, and my seeds have already been started. I am ready to transplant them to my system. In this case, I must choose the general-purpose – mild vegetative option.

4. From the basic application table, I see that I need one teaspoon (five grams) per gallon (three point seven liters) of water for the flora gro, micro, and bloom.

5. I add five teaspoons (twenty-five grams) of flora gro into the bucket and stir with a stirring stick until it has dissolved. I use five teaspoons because my solution is five gallons (eighteen liters).

6. Next, I add five teaspoons of flora micro into the bucket and stir until it is dissolved.

7. Lastly, I add five teaspoons of flora bloom to the five-gallon bucket and stir until it has dissolved.

8. After the nutrients are added, I measure the pH of the water. Most likely, the pH will be too high. You need to add a pH down solution to bring the pH between six and six and a half. You cannot add the pH down solution straight into the bucket. This will cause the nutrients to dissipate out of solution.

What you need to do is to take a cup and fill it with water from the nutrient solution. Add some pH down solution to the cup and mix it with the water in the cup. Once the pH down solution is mixed with the nutrients in the cup, pour it into the five-gallon reservoir. Measure the pH of your five-gallon mix and repeat until the pH is 6.5.

9. As a final check, I will test the TDS of the solution, and I should measure around 1000ppm + the initial reading that we took at the beginning. My TDS reading will tell me I have 1350PPM (1000PPM nutrient solution + 350PPM from my water source).

The reason for using a separate cup with the pH down solution is that it is a strong acid that can make the nutrients dissipate out of the solution. This can be seen if white crystals are forming in the nutrient mix.

Dry Nutrients

Dry nutrient mixing consists of three parts. The one I am going to talk about is the Chem-gro series from hydro-gardens.com. This is a mix that is widely used in the hydroponics community. Other mixes like the master blend or any other three-part nutrient powder mix are similar in use.

Part A

Specialized formula for the crops you intend to grow. Different recipes are available like lettuce, tomatoes, strawberries, cucumbers.

This part contains the primary macronutrients (NPK) and the micronutrients. The NPK number for the lettuce mix is 8-15-36.

Part B

Part B consists of magnesium sulfate. This contains magnesium and sulfur (sulfate), which are secondary macronutrients. Magnesium sulfate is also referred to as Epsom salt. Purchasing Epsom salt from your grocery store will be an alternative solution. Be careful to get pure magnesium sulfate without additives like smells or colors. If you want to be safe, you can order it from your hydroponics store.

Part C

The third part will be Calcium Nitrate. Calcium nitrate has an NPK of 15.5-0-0. You will have to add this to the NPK ratio of part A to get a total NPK number of 23.5-15-36. It's better to dissolve part C in warm (not hot) water to improve dissolving. Do not exceed 70°F (21°C).

How to mix a dry solution

The seller of the solutions will have guidelines for the mixing ratio. If we look at the website of hydro-gardens, we see they have a table that displays all we need to know.

Mixing instructions for chem-gro lettuce formula

CHEM-GRO LETTUCE FORMULA 8-15-36
Mixing Instructions for 100 gallons of water
(For full strength working solution)
For 1 gallon, swap out the "lbs" for "tsp" below.

Type of Fertilizer	Seedling Plants	Mature Plants
8-15-36	8 oz. / .5 lbs.	8 oz. / .5 lbs.
Calcium Nitrate (CaNO₃)	6 oz. / .375 lbs.	8 oz. / .5 lbs.
Magnesium Sulfate (MgSO₄)	4 oz. / .25 lbs.	5 oz. / .31 lbs.
pH	Adjust to 6.4 - 6.7	Adjust to 6.0 - 6.5
Conductivity	1350 ppm + source water 1.80 mhos + source water	1575 ppm + source water 2.10 mhos + source water

Nutrient mix for five gallons (eighteen liters) of water in grams: N-P-K: 8-15-35: 8 oz.=227 grams/20= 11.35 grams/5 gallons Calcium nitrate: 8 oz.=227 grams/20= 11.35 grams/5 gallons Magnesium Sulfate: 5 oz.=142 grams/20= 7.1 grams/5 gallons

This is a step by step guide on how to prepare dry nutrients:

1. Clean the residue of the previous batch.

2. Know the volume of your mixing container.

3. Fill the tank with water. Low ppm water is preferred. Do not exceed 70°F (21°C).

4. Use a stirring stick or submersible pump to move the water in a stirring motion. Measure the TDS of the base water.

5. Weigh out the correct amount of each part and put them into separate cups. For one hundred gallons, you need eight ounces of the 8-15-36 main nutrient mix, eight ounces of calcium nitrate, and five ounces of magnesium sulfate. This depends on the recommended guidelines for each manufacturer.

6. Put the powder in the solution one by one. Start with solution A and add the next part when solution A is completely dissolved. Do this until you have all three parts dissolved. Use a bucket with warm water (max 70°F or 21°C) to dissolve the Calcium nitrate (part C). When the calcium is dissolved in the warm water, pour it in the nutrient mix.

7. Measure the pH of the water and bring it down to 6 to 6.5 if need be. Use the same pH down method as I described with the liquid nutrients.

8. Check the TDS of the water. It should be around 1575ppm + the TDS you started with (source water).

Different nutrient mixes have different recommended dosages. Check the instructions the seller provides for the best results.

Liquid Vs. Powder Nutrients

There are lots of nutrient solutions on the market nowadays. Some are liquid, and some are powder. The hobbyist mostly uses liquid nutrient solutions, while powder nutrients are used for commercial or advanced growers. Nonetheless, both are very easy to make.

Liquid nutrients are more expensive than powder nutrients if you compare them to their nutrient content by weight. That's why it doesn't make sense to use liquid nutrients when you are a seasoned grower or are growing commercially.

Prices

The price of powdered nutrients will be lower than liquid nutrients. Here is the price for a five-pound nutrient mix from hydro-gardens. The total cost is

$41.85 as of October 2019. With this mix, you can make one thousand gallons of nutrient solution which is four cents per gallon without shipping.

Do you need micronutrients?

The short answer is yes. Although they are needed in much smaller quantities. Micronutrients, specifically those listed previously, are an essential part of plant growth.

If you don't supply the micronutrients your plants need, they will start to experience stunted growth, and the yield will be reduced. All 3- part liquid and dry nutrient mixes contain micronutrients.

Recommended nutrient levels

You may hear such terms as Hydroponic Nutrient Strength, TDS, PPMs, or conductivity. These are all relevant to the nutrient strength of your water, which means the better balanced these are, the happier and healthier your plants will be.

Understanding these terms will help you to maintain the perfect hydroponic system.

The TDS meter is a simple tube-like device that measures the conductivity of your water. In essence, it sends a small electrical charge through your water/nutrient mix. If there are plenty of salts and minerals, the charge will pass through it better than if it is just water.

It is important to note that electrical conductivity is measured in a unit called Siemens.

However, the amount of Siemens in your water is very small. This means we need to talk in either millisiemens, which are 100th of a siemen, or in microsiemens, which are one-millionth of a Siemens!

It will take one million microSiemens to make one Siemen.

That's why you'll see measurements ranging from 0.8 to 3 or 4 on testing gear. These are milliSiemens, the smallest measurement used in hydroponics.

An example of what this means: 0.6millisiemens is equivalent to 600 microsiemens.

Interestingly this can be declared differently in different countries. The UK may say: 'EC is 2.2', which means its 2.2 millisiemens, or 2200 microsiemens, other countries in Europe may refer to it as either of these measurements.

In the U.S., different measurements are used. They will typically talk about ppm, Parts Per Million. It's common to hear someone talking about feeding their plants at 1100 ppm. But you may also hear someone talking about their source water being under 100 ppm.

TDS means total dissolved salts or parts per million.

People in the EU use EC, which is electrical conductivity in Millisiemens.

People in the U.S. use ppm, which is TDS or total dissolved salts in parts per million.

The confusion arises because there are different ways to convert Siemens, and different solvents have different conductivity levels. We have talked about the conversion factors at the beginning of this book. This means that any measurement will be an approximation.

In effect, a TDS meter is the same as a conductivity meter. The TDS meter includes a converter to give you the reading in PPM.

In short, Europe measures the electrical conductivity in micro siemens. The U.S. could use any of the above conversion methods.

Four hundred microsiemens is the same as 0.4 millisiemens and the same as an EC of 0.4. In the U.S. this could be either of these three:

200 ppm using the NaCl conversion factor (most likely).
280 ppm using the natural water conversion factor.

220 ppm using the KCl conversion factor.

To summarize, if you're using a TDS meter, you're going to need to know which conversion factor it's using. If you don't, it will be impossible to tell if it is in the right range or not. Most of the time the conversion factor of 0.5 (NaCl) will be used.

Calibration Fluid

You can purchase bottles of calibration fluid, which are already set at 1000 ppm. The purpose of these is to allow you to verify that the reading on your TDS meter is accurate.

Of course, this means you need to know which conversion factor your meter is using.

If it doesn't show on the label, you are going to need to check with the manufacturer or possibly your supplier.

Getting the Nutrients Right

Understanding the nutrient levels in your system will take a little trial and error. It is essential to ensure your plants have enough nutrients without overdosing the system.

TDS or ppm is a guide to the concentration of specific particles in your water. It is directly affected by the pH level of your water, which means it is best to get your pH level right for your plants after you have mixed the nutrients.

Most nutrient solutions will lower the pH slightly. That's why you need to add a pH down solution after you have mixed the nutrients.

EC, TDS and pH levels

Getting the EC and pH levels right is one of the essential parts of creating a high-performing hydroponics system. The EC or TDS will depend on the mix you are using. If the company recommends using a higher TDS level for a particular crop, then follow their guidelines.

In general, you should adopt the following approach:
Seedlings: < 250 ppm or 0.5 mS + source water

Vegetating plants: 600-800 ppm or 1.2-1.6mS + source water Flowering plants: 800-1200 ppm or 1.6-2.4mS + source water

Don't forget; this is a general guide. Each plant is different, and you should balance the EC and pH levels where they work best for your plant growth.

Lettuce

pH: 6–6.5

TDS: 600-800

EC: 1.2-1.6

Tomatoes

pH: 5.5-6.5

TDS: 1200-2500

EC: 2.4-5

Peppers

pH: 5.8-6.3

TDS: 1400-2100

EC: 2.8-4.2

Pak Choi

pH: 7

TDS: 1000-1400

EC: 2-2.8

Garlic

pH: 6

TDS: 1000-1200

EC: 2-2.4

Barley Fodder

pH: 6

TDS: 500

EC: 1

Cucumber

pH: 6

TDS: 1200-1800

EC: 2.4-3.6

Cabbage

pH: 6.5-7

TDS: 1700-2200

EC: 2.4-4.4

Broccoli

pH: 6-6.5

TDS: 2000-2500

EC: 4-5

During hot weather, the plants transpire a lot of water. This will limit the nutrient uptake of the plants. It is leaving your reservoir with a TDS level that keeps on rising. You need to use a weaker solution during summer to remedy this. For lettuce, this is an EC of 0.8 in summer and 1.2 in winter.

During winter, the plants don't transpire much water, and you can increase the concentration of the solution.

Topping up nutrients

You need to keep the TDS or EC levels constant if you are topping up your reservoir with nutrients. Before you add the solution, you need to make sure it has the same EC or TDS that you started with.

If the TDS has risen, you need to use a solution that is not as strong as the one you put in initially.

If the TDS dropped, you should increase the strength of the nutrient solution.

Over-fertilizing and the death of your plants

It can be tempting to add extra nutrients to your hydroponic system. However, the assumption that it won't do any harm is false.

One of the most obvious signs that you're over-fertilizing is when your plants start to get nutrient burn. This is discoloration on the edge of the leaves.

Unfortunately, it can happen if your plant gets too much of any one of the macro and micronutrients it needs.

But, over-supplying them with nutrients is not the only reason for nutrient burn. If your plants are stressed for other reasons, they won't be able to use all the nutrients provided. This will leave them in a solution that is too rich and causes nutrient burn.

Perhaps the most common reason is when the EC levels are too high thanks to salt and mineral build-up in the water.

You should be able to see this with your PPM or EC tests.

What is nutrient lockout?

Nutrient lockout occurs when a pH adjuster is mixed in the solution. The high concentration of the pH adjuster will take dissolved nutrients out of the solution. This can be seen after you have added your pH down solution into the nutrient mix.

It can be seen if there are particles at the bottom of your container or a milky white haze in the water.

One way to combat this is if you know the amount of pH adjustment you need, to mix it at the beginning before adding nutrients. This is the preferred method.

Another way to add it is after you have added the nutrients. Use a cup (or bucket) to scoop out some of the nutrient solution and add the pH adjuster into this cup. Stir the pH adjuster around in the cup and then apply it to the nutrient mix. You are effectively diluting the pH adjuster.

Water top-ups and changes

The plants could take up the nutrients from your water reservoir slower than the water itself. This will lead to a stronger nutrient solution after a few days. If the nutrient solution is stronger than the plant likes, it is going to get signs of nutrient burn. To remedy this, you need to do a top-up of your reservoir.

That's why you need to lower your TDS or EC when the temperature increases in summer and decrease the nutrients in winter.

Top-ups are done with a nutrient solution that is half strength. The half strength will level out the EC of your nutrient solution. Sometimes, you do not need to add a half-strength solution

This is how I would recommend you to top-up your reservoir:

1. Top up the water in your reservoir to the desired level.

2. Measure the EC or TDS.

3. Depending on the measurement, you need to add the nutrient solution.

4. If the water needs more nutrients, feed them directly into your nutrient reservoir. If the EC or TDS is in the recommended range, don't add any nutrients.

If the plant takes up nutrients, it could leave other nutrients behind in the solution. This leads to nutrient accumulation in your reservoir. That's why water changes need to be done frequently. This means getting rid of the water in your nutrient reservoir and replacing it with a completely new batch of nutrients. If you were to keep topping up the reservoir, some nutrients will start to build up, and you will create deficiencies for particular nutrients. Water changes are done to remedy this.

You should do a water exchange once you have topped up the same amount of water that is the nutrient reservoir. This means if you have a one hundred gallon reservoir and you add five gallons each day, you would have to exchange the reservoir every twenty days.

$$\frac{100 \text{ gallons reservoir}}{5 \text{ gallons top up per day}} = 20 \text{ days}$$

Vegetating & Flowering Plants

Lettuce is a type of vegetating plant, while tomato is considered a flowering plant. The main difference between these types of plants is in the edible parts of the plant.

The vegetation, or greenery that grows with vegetative plants, such as lettuce, is edible. This is the part you want to cultivate.

In contrast, flowering plants, such as the tomato, don't need a vast amount of vegetative growth. Nutrients will be used to create flowers and fruits afterward.

The greater the number of flowers, the more likely it is you will have a good yield. Some people say you need a stronger nutrient mix for flowering plants. I have found very little difference between a lettuce formula and a tomato formula. Here is an example of two commercial hydroponic mixes:

Lettuce NPK: 23.5-15-36

Chem-Gro lettuce 8-15-36 (2.25 grams/gallon)

Calcium nitrate 15.5-0-0 (2.25 grams/gallon)

Magnesium sulfate 0-0-0 (1.4 grams/gallon)

Tomatoes NPK: 19.5-18-38

Chem-Gro tomato 4-18-38 (2.25 grams/gallon)

Calcium nitrate 15.5-0-0 (2.25 grams/gallon)

Magnesium sulfate 0-0-0 (1.12 grams/gallon)

We can see that the nutrient levels are very close to each other. Lettuce needs a bit more nitrate, while tomatoes need a bit more phosphorus and potassium. The macronutrients are the same, and the TDS or EC is recommended at the same levels.

While this is true for this mix (hydro-gardens.com), it might be different for other nutrient mixes. Always check the label and follow the manufacturers' guidelines. The measurements will also depend on the fact that your system is drain to waste or recirculating.

If you grow lettuce at home and would like to grow tomatoes, you don't need to get another nutrient mix. You can keep using the lettuce mix. However, if you are growing commercially, I recommend using a specialized formula for the crop you are growing. I do recommend using different nutrient reservoirs if you are going to mix lettuce and tomatoes in a commercial system.

Flushing

Flushing is used to remove excess salts from the root area of the plant. When the water uptake is higher than the nutrient uptake (in warm weather), salts are left at the root zone. This can lead to a build-up of nutrients at the roots of the plant.

You can spot this if you see white salts building upon the growing media.

You can test nutrient build-up by flushing it with a half-strength nutrient solution and checking the runoff. If the runoff is higher than the nutrient concentration you put in, it means that nutrients have built up at the root base. Continue flushing until the flushing solution is the same strength as the one you put in.

Example:

1. Take your plant and put it in a separate container.

2. Pour a half-strength nutrient mix over the root mass (500ppm).

3. Examine the strength of the nutrient solution.

4. If it is higher (500ppm+), repeat until it's lower.

5. If it is the same as the half-strength mix (500ppm), you have flushed the plant roots successfully.

Flushing can be done in dutch buckets, ebb and flow, and drip systems. Most of the time, you will cultivate lettuce or other quick turnaround crops in NFT and DWC, which do not need to be flushed.

Flushing can improve the taste of the crop. However, this is not with every crop. I recommend that you experiment with the crop you are growing, so you know if it will make a difference.

Common 3-part dry nutrient mixes

General formula per 5 gallons of water:

12 grams of 4 – 18 – 38 from Master blend 12 grams of calcium nitrate

6 grams of magnesium

Cucumber formula per 100 gallons of water

8 oz. 8-16-36 chem-gro from hydro-gardens.com 8 oz. Calcium nitrate

5   oz. Magnesium sulfate

Strawberry formula for 100 gallons of water

6   oz. 8-12-32 chem gro from hydro-gardens.com 6 oz. Calcium nitrate

4 oz Magnesium sulfate

Pepper and herb formula for 100 gallons of water

8 oz. 11-11-40 chem-gro from hydro-gardens.com 8 oz. Calcium nitrate

4 oz. Magnesium sulfate

Lettuce formula for 100 gallons of water

8 oz. 8-15-35 chem-gro lettuce formula

8 oz. Calcium nitrate

5 oz. Magnesium sulfate

Monitoring

To get the best possible yield from your plants you need to monitor the water, temperature, and humidity regularly. This will allow you to adjust and keep the system running in the best environment for the plant.

Here is what you should be checking:

Water

Your water and the nutrients are the most crucial part of your hydroponic system.

Here's what you should be monitoring at least three or four times every week, although every day is even better.

pH level

The pH level will change according to:

-The nutrients used

-The minerals in your source water

-The uptake of these nutrients by your plants

Most plants will flourish at a pH of 6 – 6.5.

If you need to lower the pH, you can purchase a pH lowering solution at your local hydroponics store. But, do not use too much, it will quickly affect the pH level of your water. Decreasing pH is done after you have added the nutrients. This is because the nutrients will already lower the pH of your water.

There are also liquids which will increase the pH of the water. However, this is not used as much because the pH of your water source will be most likely higher than 6.

Use distilled water

Distilled water has been through a process to remove the minerals in it, which could be seen as a benefit for a hydroponic system as you'll have complete control of what nutrients are in the water.

This can be especially useful if you have a water source that is very hard (400ppm+).

Hard water and soft water

The higher the mineral content, the harder the water. Naturally, hard water becomes this way as it travels through rocks and across ground that has a high mineral content. Calcium and magnesium are two of the most common minerals in hard water.

As you already know, both these minerals are required by your plants to promote healthy growth. However, water that is particularly hard has too much of these minerals for your plants.

Excess of certain minerals will result in a nutrient accumulation, the inability of a plant to access other nutrients because the high level of one or two minerals blocks the other minerals from being available.

To get the best possible results, you should aim for soft water. Water under 60 ppm is considered soft enough to cause your plants minimal if any issues.

If you do not have soft water available, you need to add the initial TDS reading to your nutrient solution.

For example:

If you start with 350 ppm and your desired nutrient solution should read 1000 ppm, you need to have a final nutrient solution of 1350 ppm.

Water temperature

While different plants prefer different air temperatures, most plants will be happy with the water temperature being between 65 and 80°F (18-26°C).

In hobby systems, you can heat the water using an aquarium heater with a built-in thermostat. In commercial operations, this is done by a natural gas water heater. Don't raise the water temperature too quickly. It will shock your plants.

If you live in an unusually warm climate, you may need to consider a water chiller in the summer. In a greenhouse, you could use an evaporate cooler to cool the temperature of the greenhouse, which in turn will cool the water. An evaporate cooler will work better in a dry climate than a humid climate.

The DWC technique is ideal for limited temperature fluctuations because of the large mass of the water. NFT systems will see significant temperature fluctuation between day and night.

Insulate growing container

It is essential to insulate your growing container as this will make a big difference to the temperature of your water and the money spent on heating or cooling.

Most people will test the water temperature and nutrient levels in the reservoir.

However, if you have extensive pipework taking the water to your growing container and the water sits in the base of your growing container, it can quickly lose heat in the colder months.

In warmer months, the opposite can happen, and the temperature can increase. Especially if evaporation is taking place, reducing the amount of water available to be heated.

Insulating your growing container can help to minimize heat loss or heat gain, which will make it easier for you to maintain the correct temperature in your system and keep the plants happy.

The easiest way to insulate a growing container is with styrofoam boards. They can be cut easily and are strong enough to put under the water reservoir without losing their R-Value (no compression).

Dissolved oxygen

In a hydroponics system, the roots may sit in water for most of their life. That's why you need to have oxygen in the water. It's known as dissolved oxygen or DO for short.

The dissolved oxygen level should ideally be above 5mg/L. Below this level, your plants are likely to suffer. Below 3mg/L, they are likely to die or suffer from stunted growth.

Adding oxygen to the water is as simple as using an air pump together with an air stone. This pumps oxygen into your water. You may want to note that the smaller the bubbles inside the reservoir, the better the oxygenation of the water. The deeper you place the air stone, the lower the volume being pumped into the water because of pressure.

However, you'll need to monitor the temperature regularly. As the water temperature rises, the solubility of oxygen decreases, effectively reducing the level of dissolved oxygen in the water.

That's why you need to add oxygen to the water and aim for a level of 5mg/L. This will ensure it stays high enough even if the water temperature rises.

If you're not sure why this is so important, just remember that oxygen gives your plant well-developed roots and increases its nutrient absorption rate. It also helps to prevent fungal and bacterial growth.

The only system you would need to supply air to is a DWC system. DWC systems can be floating rafts or bucket systems. In these systems, the roots are fully submerged.

There is no aeration needed for Kratky, ebb and flow, wick, drip, NFT, aeroponics, and fogponics.

Temperature

Ideal growing temperatures

The exact air temperature for plants will depend on what you're growing. However, most seedlings will do well in temperatures around 75°F (24°C).

Cool-weather crops

-Leafy greens

-Day time 60-70°F (15-21°C)

-Nighttime 50-60°F (10-15°C)

Warm weather crops

-Tomatoes, peppers, eggplant, cucumber

-Day time 70-80°F (21-26°C)

-Nighttime 60-70°F (15-21°C)

Plants are generally particularly sensitive to temperatures above their preferred range and will quickly suffer. You will need to monitor the air temperature regularly and take steps to maintain the air temperature. These can include:

-Adding a heater to the room

-Using a fan to increase airflow

-Use an evaporate cooler in a greenhouse

U-sing an air conditioner to reduce the temperature

Consider switching over to LED lights, which will produce less heat.

You will know if the temperature is too high as the plants will start to appear stretched, they will grow less, and may struggle to produce a yield, they will also close the stomata, making it impossible for them to transpire. This can help to retain water but increases the chance of the plant overheating and damaging its cells.

The Stomata are tiny pores in the leaves of plants. They can occasionally be found on the stems of plants. These cells are responsible for the exchange of gasses, they allow carbon dioxide into the plant for photosynthesis, while letting water vapor and oxygen out.

In general, plants will have the stomata on the bottom of their leaves, while aquatic plants, particularly floating ones, will have the stomata on the top of their leaves.

The stomata don't open and close themselves. Every stoma has two crescent-shaped guard cells that are connected. It is these that enlarge and contract, effectively opening and closing the stomata pore.

You should note that to maximize vegetative growth, you will need to keep the day and night temperature very similar. But, if you are ready to start flowering and fruiting, the night temperature should be approximately 10°F less than the day temperature.

But, too big of a difference, around 20°F, will stress your plants, reducing their ability to grow.

Humidity

Humidity is simply the measure of water in the air: the higher the water in the air the more humid it will feel.

But, how does humidity affect your hydroponic plants?

Recommended humidity

A simple humidity meter will tell you the humidity in your grow room.

If you are growing seedlings, then you need to target humidity levels between sixty and seventy percent.

However, mature plants can flourish in humidity levels around fifty percent or lower.

Effect on Nutrient Uptake

Plants absorb water all the time, especially in a hydroponics system. However, ninety-five percent of the water they consume is put back into the atmosphere. It is a process known as transpiring.

The higher the humidity level of the air, the harder it is for the air to absorb water. This effectively prevents the plants from transpiring the water into the air.

In short, if the humidity level is too high, the plants won't be able to get rid of processed water. This will prevent them from absorbing more, effectively reducing their ability to absorb nutrients.

High humidity levels will result in stunted growth and a calcium deficiency in your plants. This results in dry ends of the leaf and even rot in any blossom, commonly known as leaf rot. In lettuce, this can be seen at the center of the plant. When the edges of the leaf start to die, it means there is not enough calcium available for the plant. Instead of being a calcium deficiency, this is a humidity issue.

It is worth noting that leafy vegetables suffer particularly quickly when the humidity is too high.

Interestingly, low humidity does not tend to give as many issues.

You should also be aware that excessive humidity will encourage fungal and bacteria growth, which could be a real issue to your hydroponics system.

The best way to reduce your humidity levels is to exchange the moist air with dryer air, that is assuming the air outside the growing space is dryer. Check it with your humidity meter.

If this is the case, then allow some outside air in and release some of your grow room air. But, make sure you use bug nets on entrance points to reduce the chance of pests arriving in your growing area.

An alternative is to use a dehumidifier in your growing space. Make sure it is automatically regulated.

Don't forget that the warmer the air is, the better it is at holding humidity. If you cool your grow room with air conditioning, the humidity level will drop.

Circulating the air in your growing environment will increase plant evaporation. It will decrease the possibilities for fungus. It will increase evaporation, which will increase the growth rate of the plant.

Crop health

One of the most significant issues with hydroponic crops, or any crop, is the risk of disease or pests. Either of these can quickly destroy your hard work and leave you without a crop.

That's why it is so important to know how to deal with these issues.

Disease

There are several ways in which disease can occur or be introduced to your plants. It is essential to be aware of what these are to prevent them from becoming an issue when you are growing your crops.

Root disease

You won't be surprised to learn that root disease affects the roots of your crops. It is generally caused by a lack of oxygen getting to the plant's root, effectively making them rot. In a hydroponics system, your roots may be in the water all the time, increasing the risk of root disease.

However, providing you maintain the levels of dissolved oxygen and keep the water moving, you shouldn't have an issue with root disease.

Wash hands

Consider for a minute the number of different items you touch daily and you will quickly get an idea of the amount of dirt and contamination that you can carry unseen, on your hands.

This dirt, or bacteria, can be harmful to your plants, introducing bacteria that they don't know how to defend against. To prevent this from being an issue, you must always wash your hands or sanitize them before you enter your growing space and handle the plants or the system. Shoes and clothes are equally important.

Sanitize grow materials

A three percent bleach solution or a three percent hydrogen peroxide solution is the best way to keep the growing environment clean. Wipe every piece of equipment and surface with the solution after every harvest. This will prevent bacteria from getting to your plants and potentially killing them.

Keeping the area clean doesn't need to be difficult or time- consuming; it just needs to be consistent.

No organic material

Hydroponic systems don't use soil, which is good as soil carries hundreds of different bacteria. Many of which can be harmful to your plants.

However, just because you don't use soil doesn't mean that soil contamination can't happen. You will need to consider where your seedlings came from. If they were initially grown in soil, they are going to need to be cleaned thoroughly before being planted in the growing media.

Keeping all soil and plant material away from your hydroponic system will help to protect your plants. It is better to grow from seed instead of buying a seedling from the gardening store.

Possible Pests

Here is a list of possible pests. Afterward, I will give some tips on how to get rid of them organically.

Aphids

These tiny black or sometimes green dots can quickly suck the goodness out of any plant. They walk along the stems and suck the sap from the plant.

This removes the nutrients and will make your plant ill; eventually, it will die.

Some of the most commonly mentioned aphids are greenfly and blackfly. They can breed incredibly quickly. It is important to treat them as soon as you find them; you don't want these pests spreading over to the rest of your crops.

An aphid (can be green or black)

Caterpillars

You already know what a caterpillar is. On its way to becoming a beautiful butterfly, it will chew through every green leaf it can find.

A lettuce eating caterpillar

On the plus side, these pests are relatively easy to pick off and remove; check the underside of your leaves where they usually hide.

Squash Bugs

Unsurprisingly, these bugs are most commonly found on squash plants. They may not be an issue to you if you are not growing any squash.

They look very similar to the stink bug, are approximately half an inch long, and have flat backs. The squash bug is gray and brown with orange stripes on the bottom of their abdomen.

You'll usually find them on the underside of your leaves in a group. They can fly but generally prefer to walk on your plants. These bugs will destroy the flow of nutrients to your plants.

Mealybugs

This is yet another pest that multiplies quickly once they find a home. They tend to prefer warmer environments. Your hydroponics setup will probably be ideal for growth! The amount of damage they do will depend on the number of pests you have;

early detection is crucial. Mealybugs are oval insects approximately a quarter-inch long and covered with a white or gray wax.

Cutworms

The cutworm is the larvae of several different species of adult moths. They will generally hibernate for the winter months; unless your hydroponic system is warm enough to discourage this.

Dealing with Pests

Having a greenhouse where soil-based plants are located is a bad idea. Pests could use the soil as a breeding ground before they move on to your hydroponics setup.

Growing your produce from seed will drastically eliminate the possible pests that are on a plant. The plants you buy from your local dealer could be filled with pests already.

Sap Suckers

One of the best natural remedies for sapsuckers is to spray your plants with chili or garlic spray. However, these can affect the taste of your crop and in large quantities, can make it uncomfortable for the plants.

Moderation is the key. Alternatively, you can use beneficial insects, which are discussed later in this chapter.

Caterpillars

The simplest way of getting rid of caterpillars is to spray a substance called Bacillus thuringiensis. You should be able to get this in your local garden store.

It is a natural soil-borne bacteria that kills caterpillars and their larvae.

Mold & Fungus

Potassium bicarbonate is excellent at destroying virtually all molds and fungus. You can spray it directly onto any affected plants and the ones next to them.

Beneficial Insects

Another great way of dealing with pests in your system is to use beneficial insects. As the name suggests, these are insects that will help your system by eating the pests that do damage. It is a good idea to have them in your system year-round. That means when there will be an outbreak, they might be able to limit it or negate the outbreak.

Although it might not be easy to introduce them to your outdoor system, it is preferably done indoors or in a greenhouse where they are contained.

You can order live animals online on sites like Amazon, insectsales.com, or a local organic gardening store.

Some of the best ones to consider are:

Ladybugs

These are great at getting rid of aphids before they can do any real damage. One ladybug can consume as many as five thousand aphids per year!

This tiny wasp doesn't sting. It will lay its eggs in the body of an aphid. The baby wasp eats the inside of the aphid before emerging to repeat the process.

Praying Mantis

These slightly strange looking creatures are excellent at eating aphids, caterpillars, potato beetles, leafhoppers, hornworms, squash bugs, and pretty much any pest that could be a problem for your setup.

Lacewings

These are good at attacking virtually all types of pests. You will find they are very good at eating aphids, mealybugs, whitefly, and even thrips. They can eat as many as one hundred aphids per week. They also work best at night when most of the pests are active.

It is worth noting that if you had a one thousand square foot greenhouse, you would need approximately two thousand lacewings. You can get these from most biological insect vendors, or you can try planting flowers that attract lacewings near your system.

Good flowers to plant are fennel, dill, coriander, dandelion, and angelica.

They also like brightly-lit windows.

Spider Mite Predators

The tiny spider mite can suck the nutrients out of two hundred different plants. Fortunately, you can solve the issue by introducing the bright orange spider mite predator. They may only live for roughly forty-five days, but they can consume as many as twenty spider mites each day!

Aphid Predator Midge

These tiny little bugs look like small mosquitoes. They can sniff out aphid colonies, and then they lay their eggs next to them.

Within a few days, the larva will hatch and eat the aphids. The aphid predator midge can consume as many as fifteen aphids a day.

Nematodes

These are natural parasites that are so small you can only see them with a microscope. They can kill approximately two hundred and fifty different types of larvae.

Familiarize yourself with the most common pests in your area. Then you will know how to deal with them.

Most common problems

It feels great to get your hydroponic system set up and established, especially as the crops start to appear. However, it is essential to maintain the environment and keep an eye out for some of the most common problems.

If you catch them fast enough, you will be able to react quickly and save the plant(s).

Common deficiencies in hydroponics:

-Calcium

-Magnesium

-Iron

Other problems include:

-Chlorosis (Yellowing of the leaves)

-Necrosis - Death of the leaf

Nitrogen deficiency (N)

Yellow leaves can be a sign of a nitrogen deficiency. If nitrogen deficiency occurs, the plant will move the available nitrogen from the older leaves (bottom) to the new leaves (top). This means the bottom leaves will become yellow while the top leaves are still green. If you inspect the leaves carefully, you will see that the yellowing begins at the tip of the leaves, slowly making it's way to the center.

Phosphorus deficiency (P)

The leaves become darker, almost purple. The leaves will start to curl and will eventually drop. Phosphorus will be hard to spot at the beginning.

Potassium deficiency (K)

Potassium deficiency is also hard to spot. Older leaves (bottom) will form chlorosis (yellowing), and the edges of the leaf will turn brown with sometimes brown spots in the middle of the leaf.

The flowering of the plant is greatly diminished.

Calcium deficiency (Ca)

Calcium deficiency appears on new leaves. The edges of the leaf turn brown.

Calcium deficiency is not to be confused with tip burn (too many nutrients) or lack of airflow.

It might be possible that your plants are developing signs of calcium deficiency even when there is enough calcium in the nutrient solution. This is because the environment you are growing in is too humid. The leaves cannot transpire water, which will lead to less nutrient uptake. One of these nutrients that fails to be taken up is calcium. Calcium is used to maintain cells. If calcium is not supplied, the new leaves will turn brown on the edges.

Decrease the humidity to fifty percent and install fans to circulate the air.

Magnesium deficiency (Mg)

Deficiencies can exist four weeks before you could see it happen. The leaves at the bottom will start to yellow between the veins (interveinal yellowing) with brown spots forming on the leaves.

Over time, the leaves will almost completely turn white.

The older leaves will dry and curl up, eventually falling off the plant.

Iron deficiency (Fe)

Iron deficiency will lead to interveinal chlorosis at the new leaves (top). If you are using UV lights to remove algae from the water, you may have an iron deficiency. UV light makes iron precipitate out of the solution, making it unavailable for your plants to take up.

Too many nutrients

Too many nutrients can become a problem when you have nutrient build-up or just have added too many nutrients.

As previously mentioned, you do not want to give seedlings a full dose of nutrients. You should provide them with a quart or half of the dose of the mature plant.

Too many nutrients will result in nutrient burn, which are brown spots at the edge of the leaves. Not to be confused with calcium deficiency. The leaves will become dark green and start to curl up.

If your plants have nutrient burn, you need to flush them with a half-strength solution and lower the nutrient concentration. This is the same method we talked about in the flushing chapter.

Conclusion

One thing is certain, there is a lot of information, and it can seem incredibly confusing and complicated to run your hydroponics system.

The good news is that it isn't! The basics of a hydroponics system doesn't change, regardless of your chosen setup. For a simple Kratky setup, you would only need a container, a net pot, and seed starting cube.

Because your crop can be ready within a matter of weeks, you will be able to quickly try alternative solutions until you find the one that works best for you. As you do so, the nutrient levels, pH readings, and water hardness will all start to make sense.

In the meantime, have fun experimenting. Hydroponics isn't just a way to feed the world more efficiently. It should be a fun pastime; be open to learning more at every step of your journey.

CPSIA information can be obtained
at www.ICGtesting.com
Printed in the USA
BVHW091101251120
594186BV00012B/988